Teen-A-Pause

Consciously parenting your teen
whilst reparenting yourself

EMMA DISNEY

BALBOA.PRESS
A DIVISION OF HAY HOUSE

Balboa Press books may be ordered through booksellers or by contacting:

Balboa Press
A Division of Hay House
1663 Liberty Drive
Bloomington, IN 47403
www.balboapress.co.uk
1 (877) 407-4847

Print information available on the last page.

ISBN: 978-1-9822-8155-7 (sc)
ISBN: 978-1-9822-8157-1 (hc)
ISBN: 978-1-9822-8156-4 (e)

Balboa Press rev. date: 06/09/2020

Contents

This book is dedicated to Tom & Matilda,
thank you for teaching me the importance of
the PAUSE!

Practising the pause

Pause before reacting
Pause before speaking
Pause before behaving habitually

Pause BEFORE....

Pause and create a new way of being!

Pause... acknowledge where you are in your journey and then know that with love, self-awareness, and conscious choices you can create a better quality of life whilst supporting your teen to become interdependent and resilient.

What would make life easier for you right now in using the 'Pause?"

Parenting has been my biggest learning curve to date, I have learnt more about me and who I have become through parenting.

Teen-a-Pause stems from my first born, my stillborn Joshua, I gave birth to a little boy who would not cry, who would never ask anything of me, but for me he had to play a role in my life; otherwise all of the loss, the heartbreak and the pain would have been for nothing. I wasn't sure that becoming a parent would be a choice, I was told that I may not be lucky enough to give birth to a healthy baby.

I retrained as a psychotherapist after my loss, I wanted to ensure that my life changed, that Joshua made an impact, that I made a difference in his honour. I was fortunate enough to then have two children who felt like the biggest gifts, the most incredible blessings and I made the decision to parent 'consciously' - to be actively engaged, mentally, emotionally and physically, as much as I could. Conscious living and parenting are choices that you make in order to be aware of all that you are feeling and being, so you are not just acting out all that you know but, instead, are actively engaging in the process of change, growth and evolution. Conscious living is to love from a growth mindset! The loss of Joshua meant that becoming a parent was not a given, and due to this I wanted to ensure that I didn't take becoming a parent, or the act of parenting, for granted.

Through conscious parenting and therapy, I came to see my emotional and mental wounds, I learnt to acknowledge myself and all that I needed to ensure I was able to be as good a parent to my children as possible. Simultaneously, I started to work more with teenagers and their parents and came to realise how many parents had learnt to parent their kids from their wounds rather than their love.

We can give our kids what we never had, however they never not had that, so we don't heal ourselves, we overcompensate for our wounds through our children!

I decided to specialise in working with teenagers, I know for me, my teenage years had been the most challenging: the years when I had acted out in so many ways, the years when my parents lost the connection to me and communication with me. I felt empathy and am able to understand the teen, whilst being aware, as a parent myself, of the needs of the parental role.

Teen-a-pause is born from: Joshua- and all he has allowed me to become, Tom and Tilda and all they teach me, my teenage years of self-destruction, mental health issues, confusion, addiction and disconnection and all of the incredible teen clients and their parents who choose to get support at the most difficult of times. I honour you all for allowing me so much!

To all the parents I have worked with that I have heard say;

- 'This is not quite what you had imagined parenting to be, this is not what you had in mind when you become a parent to a newborn, how did you get here?'
- 'What is with the daily fights? The raised eyebrows the tutting? The head down and screen focussed? The silence or mumbling that answers questions?'
- 'What is it with ignoring you when you are trying to support them? Whether it is to find the easiest way to start their day, do their homework or get through challenges.'

All you want to do is ensure that everyone finds the easiest and calmest way through the day, but it seems to end up with doors slamming, shouting and the constant feeling of dread.

This is so far from what you had imagined, that it hurts, it steals your joy, your appreciation any happiness is sucked out before the day has really started. You didn't imagine you would feel so tired, so fed up, unappreciated, lost, sad and sometimes scared of what the f**k you have created in life. Being scared of the scars is a part of the journey that you will unknowingly leave on your kids, scared that you are so deeply disconnected that you don't know which way is up.

A family at war, daily conflict, relationships dislocated by the speed of everyday, realising that you have become that parent that has neglected their emotional needs, their mental health and resents so much of what is expected of you and what you have set yourself up to do. Invisible is the word that best describes you. You feel like you gave up so much to devote time to parenting and along the way you lost you. You wanted to ensure that everyone had their needs met and now they do, they want more and more. Your own needs ignored, taught by you, taught your family you have no needs. Now you carry this resentment this anger, you tolerate less, so rows erupt daily and everyone returns to their different rooms to disconnect from reality and connect to their virtual worlds.

This style of parenting is teaching teens to be their best selves when you are not!

Recognise that your child is reflecting back to you what you have not resolved within yourself!

The pages to follow will give you insights in to how to create your journey through life differently, giving you more understanding into you and your choices!

Teen-A-pause

Consciously coaching you and your kids through their teenage years and learning more about you & life as you do.

I want this book to actively engage you in the process of change; changing all that no longer serves you as you support your teen in 'becoming' all that allows them to create resilience and wellbeing.

In order to take responsibility, you must undo old habits and 'un-become' your old, negative, self, heal old wounds, and become the person you were born to be.

Where science meets emotions and parents meet teenagers, this book aims to help the ever-changing relationships in this fast-paced new world. The teenage brain is in rapid development with more chemicals rushing through it and hormones being generated than a menopausal brain.

If you are struggling, or at a loss, and have no idea what to say, or if you don't know whether tough love is in order, then this interactive and informative book compiled with the support of both teenagers and parents will help support: you, your understanding, and your choices in relation to your teen's and your own self-development through these times.

Life is a journey and we can allow each step, no matter how challenging, to support our growth in all areas, so there are numerous gifts to be found within this developmental time.

Intention of this book;
To integrate THE PAUSE into daily life and creating calmer communication

> To support and educate parents as to their teens'
> needs.

To support & educate teens through their parents to understand mental / emotional health.

To understand the teenage years as the powerful and formative transition from child to young adult, from dependent to interdependent.

To allow you to make time to reflect on where you and your teen are at this present time.

As a parent of a teen to take the time to 'unlearn' all that prevents you from being the most authentic, happy and calm you, so 'unbecoming' everything that no longer serves you, whilst supporting your teen on their journey to 'becoming!"

To Create healthier relationships both with yourself and then in turn with your teen.

Chapter 1

TMI A WORLD OF 24/7 INFORMATION

What we wish we knew before we knew it!

We are the creators of the change that we wish to feel, so it is up to us to create change!

Today's world is a fast-paced changing environment where kids are connected 24/7 if they want to be.

Connected to anyone, anywhere, there is a pressure unlike ever before to be 'seen' whether it is social media or through gaming, kids are expected, even pressurised, to create themselves in so many different arenas. In each digital world they are diluted, showing the side of themselves they believe will be accepted, liked and then feedback given by anyone, strangers alike! How crazy it must be to not really know yourself, as the teenage years are the most prolific when it comes to self-awareness and understanding, when they are learning who they are aside from all that the teen has been taught to be and to be taking their lead from a world that is distorted and so disconnected in so many ways.

It is up to us: the parents, the adults, the more experienced

1

humans, to understand what it is that the teens have to deal with. We have minimal awareness, as this is so far removed from anything we have ever known. The connectivity to technology is unlike any other time. It is a 'new world & a new way of living', so we have to become students as to how it is to live in these times. It is then up to us to cooperate and find mentally and emotionally healthy ways to integrate our worlds, learning and understandings that best support the growth of the teen, the digital native.

The teenage years are the transition from being a dependent child to becoming an interdependent young adult: it is a time of great flux, unknowns, confusion, huge neurochemical & neurobiological changes, hormonal flooding and physical growth unlike anything before. It is a time when all of the differing worlds collide: self, mental, physical, emotional, sexual, academic, friends, the past, the future and the present can all feel like a volcano on the edge of exploding, or rather imploding, and to top it all off the adults in their life are expecting them to behave in a way that is biologically impossible due to the fact that the brain is not yet fully formed...

It is up to us, the ADULT, to behave in the most appropriate, and emotionally intelligent way, when we are able to; to learn to not take their behaviour personally and teach our kids the very important lessons that allow them to be emotionally and mentally aware, resilient, stable and connected, firstly to themselves and then to whatever feels healthy.

How we grew up required very different skills and ways of being compared to those that are needed today, we were allowed to grow at a completely different pace, as life was lived in such a different way. They are 'digital natives' and we are not.

YOU ARE THEIR PARENT, you may share friendship but the first relationship with your teen is as the guide, coach, boundary creator, role model, connector, confident, arguer, teacher, taxi driver, banker, support worker, healer and cheer leader.

You are their anchor!

Your role is to be able to listen, accept, argue, forgive, unconditionally love, create calm order and balance, to see them especially when they cannot see themselves clearly, to hold space as they 'become' more of whom they want to be, to acknowledge their uniqueness whilst honouring them and to witness their world compassionately. They may challenge you and all you stand for and against, they will question your way of being and it is for you to learn with them. Maybe there is no right or wrong, rather a 'new' way of seeing and being!

Be the adult you want your child to become

Parenting is the most important job we do and yet it is the one that we get the least support, education and understanding for and with, in fact sometimes it can feel like no matter what we are faced with, we don't feel like we have the time, resources, capacity or awareness.

It is a learning journey and one we can grow through and with.

THEY ARE THE TEEN and their journey is one where they are working with so much in development, mentally, physically & emotionally, they are not fully created on the inside yet to the outside world the changes may appear small. It is a massive time of changes within every area of their life!

The teenage brain is going through the most massive development, it is still under construction (there is a whole chapter on this as it is so fundamentally important to the understanding of this journey). Chemically & hormonally their bodies are going through shifts that would look like the most massive earthquake ever, off the Richter Scale entirely, with constant tremors.

They are also experiencing people in life in such different ways, so mentally & emotionally they are being challenged – being asked every day in one way or another – WHO ARE

YOU? WHAT DO YOU STAND FOR? OR AGAINST?
HOW ARE YOU, YOU? ARE YOU WITH US? ARE YOU
DIFFERENT? DO YOU FIT IN? DO YOU WANT TO?

So perhaps some very simple questions may start this process
of connection in times of challenges. Talk to them in a way that
feels comfortable, so perhaps an email, text or message to start
the chats and then when the teen feels more at ease begin to
integrate some form of presence. That presence can be whilst you
are driving, walking or in a place where eye contact is minimal,
as this can initially feel awkward and immediately makes some
conversations feel attacking.

Simple questions can open up your teen to talk;

- How are you feeling mentally? Physically? Emotionally?
- How are you thinking?
- What is good in your world?
- What is challenging?
- What can we do to support you at this time?
- What do you want from me/us?
- What will make this feel different?
- What do you need to manage/ get through this?
- What will this time look like when you are the other side?
- Are there are any things you can learn from this to help
  you grow?
- Why do you think this is happening?
- Is this having an impact in ways we can't see?
- How is this affecting you?
- Is there anything we are doing to add to the situation?
- What is the best possible outcome? How will that look?
  Feel?

It can be very helpful on the journey of change to have a
journal to jot notes down in, as part of the process of change

is firstly to become aware of the situation or behaviour and to recognise what it is that you want to change, to upgrade and then to become aware of how this situation plays out. You must have the intention to consciously and actively do something different to allow for these changes to occur, just to become aware is not enough.

Now to practise the new behaviour!

Working daily with teens teaches me so much about how it is, so many teens find communicating especially hard with their parents, as we as parents don't always listen well or pay attention to all that is being said. I have found that the easiest way sometimes is an email where you let the teen share and then ask them what it is that they need in the way of support, is it to listen? Or share advice? Or something more? If we ask them, we are empowering them as to what will allow them to deal with the situation. Many parents react in such a way that closes the teen down, or the parent might then bring it up regularly. So again, **ASK!** 'Let me know when you want to check in with this again?' is a great way of checking in.

I recently worked with a teen who struggled with low moods and no motivation, he had found out that a family member had serious health issues and instead of asking about the reality, as he did not want to upset people, he had spent quite a few months overthinking and had been unable to sleep and eat properly and had ended up feeling depressed, lost and completely disconnected. The solution was to explore his feelings and to find ways for him to communicate in a way where he did not feel too vulnerable, expressing his worst fears whilst exploring the best case too.

Emma Disney

Space for notes:

Ideas & Insights

Every teen and every parent are unique, so there is no perfect way to parent and there is no such thing as a perfect parent or teen, so perhaps we should aim for: **good enough, calm enough, open enough, connected enough.** If we take the pressure off ourselves, we too, in turn take the pressure off our teen!

The quality of your life is directly related to the quality of you and your:

- Thoughts
- Words
- Food
- Sleep
- Health
- Purpose
- Environment
- Relationships

Ideas to support you as a parent:

1. Make time for you in your day
2. Check in with yourself daily
3. Create calm in your head, 'headspace'
4. Listen to what you need in order you can then hear your teens needs
5. Be open, to learn with and from your teen
6. Be honest about your shortcomings and grow together
7. Recognise you in your teens behaviour and own it
8. Allow yourself to 'feel' life
9. Own all of your feelings and don't be scared by them
10. If you want your teens to talk and share, talk and share
11. Get your teens to be part of the 'team' build their awareness
12. Notice what is about your teen that triggers your reaction

13. Be aware of when you are behaving 'unconsciously'
14. Look at your behaviour as you look at your teens
15. Be compassionate to yourself and your teen
16. Stop judging and controlling yourself
17. Start accepting all that you are and how far you have come
18. Allow yourself to be 'happy' create happy!
19. Look for the good in people, situations and daily life, recognise GOOD
20. BE GRATEFUL, teach gratitude, role model appreciation

We are all **winging it** we are all trying to fit in, feel good, be more, allow more. The world we live in today is the fastest changing ever due to technology, it is for us to allow it to enhance us, for us to make choices as to how we invite it in.

At present we are being overwhelmed by the speed of life with expectations of 24/7 living and communicating, the fact that we **can** be connected all of the time does not mean we **have** to be. We can be connected too: information, people and knowledge every minute of every day but we are the ones that have to recognise THE BOUNDARIES, THE POWER OF NO, CALM & QUIET AND THE IMPORTANCE OF MENTAL HEALTH....

Just because we are able to do something, does not mean we have too, take a moment before you say YES and become aware if that YES will cost you your CALM!

Taking time for ourselves to review what's going on for us and how we are managing, allows us headspace to be present in our lives – what does this mean?

It means to be fully awake mentally and emotionally, not to be on automatic or cruise control as life can become a collection of habits of things we do just because we have always done them.

We deserve more for and from ourselves, as do our teenagers and when we live in being more present, more conscious, we teach them too.

It is so easy as we get older to stop learning and growing, to get 'stuck' and to feel as if life is a relentless 'to do' list. Through this we suck the joy out of ourselves and therefore our lives. We become lost in our chores, overwhelmed in the responsibilities, and life can become hard work. We have choices, we always have choice, it is for us to make the time to invest in how we choose to live our life.

When we are planning a journey we decide where to, what route, when, how, what mode of transport and then we ensure we have all that we need to carry out the plan. With life it is not quite as simple, but we can stop on a regular basis, pull into a lay-by and review our route, reflect on where we are, how we are and what would enhance our journey. We live more consciously and from a place of empowered choices and this in turn teaches our teen about their power, bravery, courage, choices and growth.

So much of who we are, how we are, what we are, and who we have become unconsciously, learned behaviour. We learn as we go along, we learn as we need too, we learn from our mistakes, we learn from understanding or feeling what we don't want as well as what we do want.

I wonder how our lives would be if we were to invest significant time, energy and commitment in to learning how to be more emotionally and mentally well.

Many people invest time and money in gym memberships, golf clubs, nights out, new clothes, shoes and holidays in order to 'feel' good but only a small amount of people invest in therapy or emotional learning and healing. One of the most powerful ways to feel good, is to look at what has us feeling disconnected from ourselves, to look at the wounds within.

To invest in healing ourselves allows for us to be more present, as well as being able to witness, nourish and parent our children consciously and with intent.

Maybe therapy feels too much: reading, sharing, talking writing it out. Each and every one of us has wounds from our childhood, emotional and mental pain that we have grown from and within. It is for us to not pass on to the next generation the behaviours, the defended attitudes and reactions that prevent us from being brave, courageous and creating the life, the family, the dreams we have! It is about UN-BECOMING all that no longer serves us!

Let us recognise the gifts in each moment, in each teen, in every interaction because one day your teen will be an adult who no longer lives with you or needs your support, whose time becomes a treat, who has the choice to see you or not, so create a relationship that enhances both of you.

When we invest in the gift of the present moment, we live from love and awareness!

Space for notes:

Virtual, Technology & Reality

'Digital Natives' is what today's teenagers are, they have not known a world without technology as many of us parents have. Their world, lives and days are shaped, often led and perhaps consumed by technology in one way or another!

It is for us to shape a path with technology, so it supports and enhances them and our relationships as opposed to it becoming an antagonistic 'battle.'

There are many benefits to technology, along with its risks, and it is for us to model, guide and create healthy boundaries as to what importance we place on the role that technology plays in our teens' life.

It is similar to allowing younger kids sweets; you would not leave out a huge selection and say help yourself whenever you want, you allocate boundaries, expectations and educate them on the effects!

Benefits of technology:

- Access to information
- Maintain and support friendships
- Create and support identities and understanding of self
- Connection, sense of belonging to peers and differing communities
- Escapism, a place to use your imagination

It is up to us to educate our teens as to what it means to use social media and technology to support themselves as opposed to 'self -harm', hide or disconnect.'

Risks of technology:

- Cyber bullying – it is too easy for kids to become vulnerable where the internet is concerned. Create regular conversations, no matter how awkward, to know what your teens are doing online and if necessary, find a way where you have permission to access their information with them.
- Trolling – when people deliberately bully, undermine or try to upset others though internet.
- Isolation – teens can use technology to escape the challenges of the real world, however this can only lead to mental health issues. Finding a balance and realistic time boundaries that are adhered to helps with clarity.
- Inappropriate material and relationships – unless we speak with our teen about expectations, appropriateness, age restrictions they can be looking at and affected by information, images and connected to people that traumatise, negatively impact and affect the mental and emotional wellbeing of our teen.
- Addiction & Mental health issues – many kids are spending too much time at a screen they are finding everyday life challenging, and mental health issues can arise.

We don't leave our front door open for anyone to walk through, we secure and protect our home. Your teens mind is their first home, why are we not protecting it with more awareness and education and what they need.

Adolescence is the most precious and expansive time for the brain, a time when it requires greater care, safeguarding and understanding.

To understand what feels right for you is to question your beliefs and understandings before the conversations start:

- Is it ok for your teen to play games above their age restriction?
- Do you mind your teen posting 'selfies' what are the boundaries?
- How long a day is your teen allowed to be on screen?
- Are screens allowed in all rooms at all times?
- Are there rooms/times/places where screens are band?
- Do you know who your teen follows?
- Do you know who they communicate with?
- Do you have access to your teens' phone/laptop?
- What role do you want social media to play in their life?
- Do you talk and share with them as to what they get from it?
- Are you aware of your 'phone' habits? Do you have limits for you?
- What are they using screen time for distraction? Procrastination? Escape?
- Have you have had a family screen time audit?
- Could you and your teen take 'screen breaks'
- What role would you like technology to play in your family life?
- Do you play 'connect' with your teens gaming life?
- How could you make technology more family connective?

If we can find a healthy balance for ourselves and then with our teen, we can support them in using technology to enhance their lives but not to be their whole life.

It is our job to ensure that we are role modelling what we expect from our teens.

BALANCE reality and technology!

We are aware that social media plays a huge role in most teens' life but is it because technology plays a huge role in parents' life?

Is technology the toddlers' security blanket, is it a place of distraction and escape?

Are we teaching our kids to be present elsewhere? Everywhere but in the reality of life?

Is it that we are the teachers of disconnection? Are we not distorting life by having created virtual babysitters? And then when it suits us wanting our teens to interact as and when we choose.

Technology and social media are addictive, and the teenagers' brain are highly sensitive to this.

Every time social media is checked, a text comes in, Facebook is checked or a snapchat alert comes through, the addictive chemical in the brain, dopamine is released, it is the same chemical that is released when smoking, drinking or gambling, that is how addictive social media is. Dopamine is released and there is a numbing in the brain that then becomes hard wired, so we have encouraged, paid for and created an addiction to a device that is life changing.

It is vital that we create strict, loving and healthy boundaries, whether that is no phones in certain rooms, or at times, for them to be charged downstairs and that there is a healthy amount of time without a phone, for both you the parent and the teen!

Then there is space to connect, to build real relationships, to get lost in daydreams, lookout the window, be bored, be creative and be engaged in life.

Reality

Today's world is so very different from the one most of us, parents', grew up in. The biggest change is technology and how connected we all are, how the world has become smaller in an instant! In a matter of decades daily life, the very basics, have been changed beyond all recognition, the speed of development of technology and social media means this is only escalating. Our teens have the power and insight to know within seconds an event that is taking place the other side of the world and when a discovery takes place as it is discovered. Technology is incredibly powerful, it also works to make the world so small that technology can bring, people, places and situations into your life, that we had the luxury of leaving outside before the internet. It so much harder in every way to close the door on the outside world, mentally, physically and emotionally as it rests in their hands through their phones! Before we explore further the pros and cons of the virtual world and it impact on this generation, let us remind ourselves what they need from the 'REAL' world.

What are the basic needs that we, humans, require in order to survive and then to thrive?

The "human givens."

Emotional needs include:

- Security -safe territory and environment which allows us to develop properly
- Attention – to give and receive it
- Sense of autonomy and control
- Being emotionally connected to others
- Being part of a wider community
- Friendship, fun, love and intimacy
- Sense of status within social groupings
- Sense of competence and achievement
- Meaning and purpose – which comes when we are being stretched in what we do, create and think.

The resources we have to help us meet these needs include:

- The ability to develop complex long-term memory, which enables us to learn and grow
- The ability to build rapport and connect to others
- Imagination, which allows us to focus our attention away from emotions and be more creative with problem solving
- A conscious rational mind that can check out emotions, questions, analyse and plan
- The ability to understand the world unconsciously, through pattern matching
- An observing self, the part of us that can step back and be more objective and rationalise – THIS PART is still in development in the teens brain!
- A dreaming brain that allow us to defuse and release the emotions of the day that have not been worked through.

Basic Human Needs for Emotional Health & Wellbeing

How well are your needs met?

For good emotional health and wellbeing your basic needs have to be met, in a way that is appropriate for you.

Basic Human Need	Examples	How well is it currently met? (Score1 = not at all, 10 = fully met)	How will you better meet this need in future?
The need to feel understood and connected	Sharing ideas, feelings and dreams with others.		
The need to give and receive attention	Regular contact with other people.		
Physical Health	Exercise, nutrition, sleep.		
Having a sense of control	An appropriate sense of control in your life, letting go of the things outside of your control.		
Need for creativity and stimulation	New challenges, learning and expanding your horizons.		

The need for purpose and goals.	Making future plans or having a sense of purpose.		
A sense of connection to something bigger than oneself.	Religion, community groups, Voluntary work. Anything that takes the focus off yourself.		

www.humangivens.com The Human Givens Approach Joe Griffin and Ivan Tyrrell

We have all that we need to survive within ourselves. It is learning with all that is going on around us, in this ever- changing environment, how best to develop, learn, support and give our teens the skills and the understanding that is difficult. To not just survive but to **THRIVE**.

When we are feeling emotionally fulfilled and are operating with ease within our world, we are more likely to be mentally healthy and stable.

When too many of our physical and emotional needs are not met, or when we use our resources incorrectly, we can suffer distress, both mentally and emotionally. Which has as effect on us physically and those around us.

It is another area where we as parents need to be on our game, so we can model what this looks like. Our teens will do all that we do, no matter what we say, they unconsciously learn their habits, their behaviour and how to be them by watching us, learned behaviours!

How well are your needs met and how does this affect you when life gets tough? How resilient are you?

Space for notes:

Chapter 2

THE RESTRUCTURING ARCHITECTURE OF THE TEENAGE BRAIN AND ITS IMPACT

Brain & Behaviour – beginners guide to the teenage brain, neuroscience

I am **NOT** a neuroscientist in any sense of the word but having worked with thousands of teenagers over the years there are many common traits that tie in to their differing behaviours. I began to see and feel that it could not be coincidence, there had to be a perfectly good reason for seemingly great kids turning in to high risk takers. Teens who although intelligent and perhaps street wise on numerous occasions acted without what appeared to be rational thinking, or awareness of the consequences, repeating the same mistakes, whist never seeming to understand or notice that they were replicating the same behaviour and not learning from it.

I had heard so many parents challenged by the daily behaviour of their teens, the smallest of things from not being ready for school at the necessary time, or not tidying up after themselves, it's not usually the big stuff that creates the battles, it is the everyday stuff, the routine of life and living, the teenage years of dependence to interdependence!

Let me share the neuroscience in its most basic form, as that is how I have learnt to understand and use it with my family, my clients and their parents.

The teenage brain is not fully formed, in fact the brain is not fully developed until 25.

Recent research has found that the adult and teen brains work differently. Adults think with the prefrontal cortex, the brain's rational part. This is the part of the brain that responds to situations with good judgement and awareness of long-term consequences. The adult brain has the capacity for executive functioning. Whereas teens process information with the amygdala, part of the limbic system which is responsible for emotions, survival instinct and memory. Your teen is thinking and processing life from the emotional part of their brain.

"In teen's brains, the connections between the emotional part of the brain and decision making are still developing and not necessarily at the same rate. That is why when teens experience overwhelming emotional input, they can't explain later what they were thinking. They were not thinking as much as they were feeling."- **Rochester University, New York**

The frontal lobes take the longest to develop and these are the areas that are vital when it comes to awareness of consequences and behaviour. The teens' brain is a bit like a car without brakes, they don't have the necessary neurological equipment to act in a way that is 'responsible' therefore it is our job to know how to help them with the equipment they do have. With this awareness and a brain that IS fully formed, we have a responsibility to **<u>PAUSE</u>** and respond not react to our teen and their behaviour, their choices and the consequences. It requires us to have compassion and new levels of understanding to guide the teen through a time of great choices, maybe alongside incredible changes that can become overwhelming challenges without the right back up and knowledge to hand.

It is for us to educate ourselves and then in turn our teen. We can choose to meet their emotions, their reactions with our calm, our wisdom!

You are the most important role model they have, the way you behave, fulfil your responsibilities and respond to them is how they learn to behave. It becomes their foundation for behaviour, in therapy we call it 'learned behaviour', and it has a long- lasting impact on your teen.

The most effective way to work with your teen and their developing brain is to set up the awareness so it is a known habit. Create a thought process, thereby establishing the neural pathways as opposed to relying on the structure of the brain to do the job it can do when fully developed, but not when in development. It is very similar to using the gears in a car to slow down when the brakes are not working!

Creating an alternative route but to the same destination, we as the parents play the role of the satellite navigator, to set up and guide whilst the teen observes and recalls the journey or pattern. Methods such as:

- **'Discussing the consequences of their actions** can help teens link impulsive thinking with fact. This helps the brain make the connections and wires the brain to make the link more often.
- **Remind your teen that they are resilient and competent**. As they are so focused in the moment, teens have trouble seeing they can play a part in bad situations. It can help to remind them of times in the past that they believed would be devastating but turned out for the best.
- **Become familiar with things that are important to your teen**. Showing an interest in things they are involved in shows them they are important to you.

- **Ask teens if they want you to respond**, when they come to you with problems, or if they just want you to listen.'
University of Rochester, Medical Centre, New York

The way we think is how we have been taught to think, so parents are the teens first teachers. If as a mother you are a worrier, or worst-case thinker, or as a father, you are a 'fixer' your teen has learnt this style of thinking from you.

Take the time to become aware of how it is your brain works with regards to differing situations and see if you can find ways to upgrade your thinking styles, just like you upgrade your phone!

Our brain is a pattern matching organ that seeks to match our experiences to pre-existing templates to make sense of the world. When we understand and start to make sense of this we can begin to see where our brain makes automatic associations, some which do not support us. Patterns therefore need to be supplemented by associative learning, which as parents is an important part of guiding the development of the teens, brains, behaviours and choices. Broadly speaking the brain does two things; it processes inputs from our body and world and generates outputs to muscles and internal organs in response.

Understanding the brains development is vital in understanding the teens behaviour, so I am going to explain it again differently, as I believe as a parent if I can fully grasp this (and I am still very much in the practical process of this with my two teens) then I can change how I parent and how I am able to find that extra love and patience that is needed at this time.

The brain is still very much under construction and the most massive remodelling occurs during the teenage years. The brain develops from the back to the front, so the last area of the brain to be developed is the pre-frontal cortex. This is the part of the brain that is responsible for executive function

23

- Goal setting
- Paying attention
- Motivation
- Planning
- Understanding consequences
- Self-control

With the pre-frontal cortex not fully developed it then becomes fully understandable that the teen is not able to behave as we might expect them to; this part of the brain is still being built.

The teen acts from a place of emotions not from a place of rationality, which explains why reactionary impulsive behaviour can be seen more at this time.

The brain is also more vulnerable to addiction at this time, as the reward centre is highly active and super sensitive, which is why peer pressure can play a massive role in teens and their behaviour. Teens are more impulsive and take higher risks due to the brains developing nature. This also impacts on emotional responses, your teen may appear more dramatic because they are experiencing emotions very dramatically, some emotions, they may be feeling for the first time. The neural development at this time is one of the most powerful times ever and as a parent and adult whose brain is fully developed it is our responsibility to be aware of how to navigate these times in the most supportive, responsive and loving ways! From dependence to interdependence!

If you want to learn more go to YouTube and see:

Nathan Mikaere Wallis on teenage brain development

Professor Sarah-Jayne Blakemore The Mysterious workings of the Adolescent brain

I have researched so much about the teenager's brain and the major insights that have impacted me, my parenting and my work is that I no longer believe that kids misbehave intentionally.

Teenagers can only do as well as they can, given their current brain development and whether their physical, emotional and mental needs are being met appropriately. These facts are the reason why so many kids struggle through their teenage years.

Space for notes:

Sleep, Exercise & Nutrition

Sleep is the most important aspect of our health and during the teenage years this plays a massive role in mental health, neural growth and emotional wellbeing. Now is the time to understand what the impact of good sleep does to build and support the teen and then the consequences of lack of sleep.

What does sleep mean to the teen?

- The teen brain is, as discussed earlier, going through massive structural changes and these occur during 'sleep.' 'Pruning' takes place, this is the process where the brain develops a leaner and more efficient way to be, maturation.
- Sleep is the glue that allows us to reconnect to experiences and to remember everything we have learned that day.
- Memory and learning are thought to be consolidated during sleep.
- Sleep not only consolidates memories but also prioritises them by stripping them down into their components and then organising them according to their emotional importance.
- Sleep plays a massive role in how teens manage stress.
- The more you learn the more sleep you need, as the brain needs the time to integrate the information.
- One of the major changes in the teen brain is the timing of the release of the sleep hormone, melatonin research has shown that this is not released until 10.30pm, which means teen find it harder to fall asleep earlier. A delay of sleep timing occurs in the teens brain.

Neuroscientists have discovered that in order for the teen brain to be able to function at its best it needs 9 hours sleep. The sleep hormone melatonin is not released until 10.30 and then going to school requires the teen to rise between 6-7.30 a.m. then you have a teen regularly working from a sleep deprived mind. The lack of sleep in turn plays a major role in the teen's mental health and emotional wellbeing, add into the mix that the teen is living from their most emotional part of their brain and you have all the ingredients for a daily earthquake if not volcano.

Professor Matthew Walker has written the book 'Why We Sleep', and within this book he states that sleep is the most significant factor when it comes to the brains' development, it is pivotal to the way the brain matures in its thinking and reasoning ability. An insightful book to invest in to learn more about the power of sleep for the teenage brain.

What happens when teens don't get enough sleep?

The impact is huge ranging from rise in blood pressure, skin conditions, poor diet as they crave carbohydrates and sugar in order to get a quick fix of energy, injuries in sport due to changes in awareness and coordination. Emotionally, it affects their moods, self-esteem, they are less tolerant and patient, the teen can find handling their emotions overwhelming, therefore they can be more reactive, aggressive and unable to self-regulate.

The brain is unable to function to its highest level, so not only is it being pruned and growing now with lack of sleep, learning becomes more difficult, concentration is seriously affected, creativity impacted and the teen's memory and problem solving is increasingly impaired. It can be seen that the role of sleep is critical in teens development; when it is lacking it impacts on every area of a teens' life. Mental health issues tend to appear within the teen years and sleep may play a pivotal role in how we can support and manage this.

How can we as a parent support the teen to get better quality and more sleep?

- Create a bedtime habit with them, the brain loves patterns and routines allow the brain a way of recognising what is to come.
- Together decide on a bedtime, appropriate to allow teen to get enough rest.
- Explain the importance of sleep and remind them of the power of sleep, like a bank account, the sleep you get today enhances the brain you are building as an adult
- No screens at least 90 minutes before bed – unless your teen is anxious and then a screen can be a distraction from their head.
- Calm time leading into bedtime – it is your responsibility to create this so what do you need to allow this to happen?
- If your teen has worries, get them to talk earlier in the evening.
- Writing down worries, to do lists what to get ready for the next day before wind down time is really helpful to empty the brain.
- Reading in bed, listening to book, gentle music.
- Keep the bedroom as much as is possible just for sleep and relaxing.
- Taking the pressure off going to sleep is important, relaxing is also beneficial

Exercise

Is an important part of keeping teens healthy, encouraging a healthy lifestyle is important, mentally, physically and emotionally; The benefits of physical activity;

- Create a healthy relationship with and for your body

- Has a powerful affect and impact on the brain
- Improves circulation throughout the body
- Boosts energy levels
- Releases tension
- Improves self- image
- Helps manage stress
- Fights anxiety and depression
- Increases enthusiasm and optimism
- Increases muscle strength
- Creates a healthy routine
- Supports a healthy lifestyle long term

Exercise plays a massive role within the brain and its continual development. Exercise has been proven to be one of the most transformative ways to support and impact how our brain works and how we feel. It effects the prefrontal cortex and the hippocampus, both of which play a role within our daily lives. The prefrontal cortex as discussed earlier controls our decision making, planning, attention, focus and personality and the hippocampus our ability to retain long term memories. Exercise allows for both of these parts of the brain to grow. Exercise has immediate impact as it increases the level of neurotransmitters that are mood changing, improving our ability and shifting our attention. Exercise also has a long-lasting affect as it changes the brain in its structure and its function.

Not all kids want to play sport or enjoy PE and games at school and that is understandable, however there are so many ways to get exercise. From running or walking to bike riding, skating, swimming, tennis, basketball, gymnastics, yoga, rock climbing, skipping – there are different ways to introduce exercise, it can be enjoyed alone, or you can support your teen to get fit.

Technology has become one of the top past times for teens and it is creating a generation who do little or no exercise due to the amount of time spent attached to a screen. This will have long lasting impact on their mental and physical health. It is our responsibility to ensure that exercise becomes a part of their lifestyle. Exercise plays a vital role physically in how our body, looks and feels, as well as how mentally we are able to support our brain to work and think its best. Emotionally it changes our moods and releases the neurochemicals that impact how we feel.

In order to support our teen to be able to develop at their best it is vital that we help them to create a lifestyle that supports good quality and quantity of sleep and has adequate exercise to build the healthiest brain and body. Both of these can be used as preventative tools for mental and emotional wellbeing. We have become aware that between 8-9 hours sleep is vital and neuroscientists are saying that at least 3-4 thirty minutes slots of aerobic activity a week is also beneficial.

Nutrition

Sleep and exercise play vital roles in the teen and their development in many differing ways, and the other major contributor is food, the fuel that supports the teen to give them the energy they need to be able to live the best 'quality' of life physically.

It can be said that 'food is love in action' what we feed and teach our children about food is how we teach them to feed and nourish themselves for life. Food is our battery charger, no teen is ever without a charged phone, so let's also teach them that in order to have the right kind of energy they have to understand the power of food. Good food can create a good mood, just as easily as junk food in can support and create a bad mood and mood swings. The teenage brain is fast growing, changing and developing and it requires a certain amount of fuel to feed it in order for it to be nourished.

As a parent our relationship with food will have a direct impact on the teen as they pick up habits, acquire tastes and learn about the importance, or lack of, from us, their role models. It is important then, that we make our relationship with food more conscious. We too will have learnt our attitudes from our family, and they can have a lasting impact as to how we feel about food, mealtimes and the value of food to our life.

A mother on a constant diet will unconsciously teach her daughter all of her insecurities about her body and food, whilst a father who may not take any responsibility for what he eats, or his health again teaches their teen.

We must show our kids how to be much more than we tell them.

A teen's mind and body continually grow, so it requires eating well, the right nutrients and the right balance of food. All food can be enjoyed, it is just ensuring the right amount of certain foods are consumed so that they do not have a negative impact. In short it is about eating healthy, more of the nutrient rich food and less of the foods and drinks high in fat, sugar, caffeine. The right food supports a teen to stay happy and calm. Keep it simple

What is good for the teen:

- Fresh fruit and veg – 5 portions daily
- Protein – fish, eggs, white meat and red meat x2 weekly, nuts and cheese
- Carbohydrates – rice, pasta,

To limit:

- Sugar – in all its forms, sweets and drinks
- Caffeine – energy drinks, teas and coffee
- Processed food – full of chemicals and has an impact on hormones

Take time to reflect on how you relate to food and the relationship you have with it:

- What is your relationship to food?
- Do you eat for pleasure or fuel?
- How well do you eat?
- How do you feel about your eating lifestyle?
- What would you like to change?
- How could you make the changes?
- What do you wish you had been taught about 'nutrition'?

If we educate our kids as to the necessary building blocks to make for a happier, easier life then, we are empowering them to create themselves; to be more resilient, confident, self- assured, self- reliant, independent and healthier.

A great way to encourage a teen to understand the value of food is to teach them to cook, to inspire them to want to learn about their bodies, along with getting them to watch the documentaries that have been made with regards to 'junk food' and its negative impact.

When we empower our teen, we support them to become their best selves!

Success is not about money, fame or a big house, it is about becoming the best version of YOURSELF.

Space for notes:

The Pause...

"Between stimulus and response there is a space. In that space is our power to choose our response. In our response lies our growth and freedom."- Man's Search for Meaning, Viktor Frankl

Imagine the times you have thought...'if only I could have done that differently' whether it is with yourself, your partner, friend or most importantly with your teen. A lot of time these situations occur as we are reacting from our feelings, a knee jerk reaction and one that can become habitual. We can also recognise that some of these reactions are how we were parented, and although we may not have appreciated it as a teen, we have just continued the pattern, you know that time when you realise you are more like one of your parents than you care to admit.

How about we use mindfulness, our mindset, the power of creating new habits and the most incredible 'super-computer' we have access to, our brains, to choose to **just do one thing differently.**

Let us look at what the pause allows us to the power to do;

o Stop
o Take a moment
o Calm – count to 10/100/1000 if necessary
o Take your power back – instead of acting out of pure emotion and potentially over reacting
o Integrate emotions and thoughts
o Evaluate
o Look at options available
o Recognise habitual behaviour
o Make choice as to what will make the situation different
o Choose to **RESPOND** not react
o Enhance our connections by being actively engaged

o Become our teens back up not enemy
o Be the safe place, where our teen knows they are heard
o Teach our teen we may not agree but we can talk through and allow them 'open mindedness'
o Become more of the parent we wish we had experienced
o Allow ourselves space

When we look at creating and introducing the **"PAUSE"** within ourselves, and our parenting, we are allowing ourselves;

- to most importantly role model to our teens that there is always a choice in how situations can be dealt with
- to make informed choices in emotional situations
- to be able to trust oneself and to deal with any situation
- to create stronger more consistent relationships with our teens
- recognise habits that no longer work
- change a way of being
- heal old ways that have hurt us
- recognise our feelings and feel them, not react to them
- take time out to be 'different' thereby teaching teens you always have the power to grow therefore creating a growth mindset.

Life can be the most incredibly powerful learning curve if we let it!

It can also be relentless due to our patterns of behaviour. We can get trapped because the habit is what we have always known and so we continue generations of behaviours that are ingrained through us, as opposed to our chosen authentic behaviour. Every day we can learn from all that happens and in order to do so we have to make time to reflect and pause so that we have the space to be, do and act differently.

The PAUSE is not just a tool for more engaged parenting, it can be a tool that allows us to engage with ourselves and recognise how much of us is a pattern, because we have always done it this way. When we create time to pause, we create space to reflect on how we are who we are, how our choices shape our lives and then we can choose after recognising these elements to create new patterns and establish new habits that support us in the here and now. This all takes time, but the investment is life changing for both ourselves and those around us, so our teen is impacted by these choices.

What would make life easier for you right now in using the 'Pause'?

'Practising the pause
Pause before reacting
Pause before speaking
Pause before behaving habitually
Pause BEFORE....
Pause and create a new way of being'

For me as a parent, the pause has become what allows me to create space when I feel overwhelmed, hurt or disappointed. The pause allows me to stop and not react with anger, it allows me to stay connected to my son or daughter, as opposed to my emotional wound! The pause buys me time to respond and not react, it allows my relationship to my teen to be loving and kind.

Space for notes:

Rational & Emotional

'What we think we become.'
Buddha

How we think determines how we manage life and yet we are never really taught how to think. We pick it up in the same way we pick up learning our native language, by absorbing how those around us think, and if we are lucky enough, we have numerous people who think in many differing ways with which to learn from and with.

The way your teen thinks will affect and impact;

o   how they learn
o   how they see the world
o   how they navigate through life
o   how they manage people
o   how they feel stress and the daily requirements needed to survive and then thrive.
o   the ability to recognise and support them to 'think' differently
o   keeping an open mind, allowing them more strategies.

One of the most important facts to remember and I will remind you again, is the teenage brain is not fully developed, so the part of the brain as I have mentioned earlier that is used for 'executive function': planning, focussing, organising and being aware of consequences is not actually fully formed. Your teen is thinking from their 'emotional brain.'

Take a moment to actually recall a time when you have made a decision, and we have all done it, from the most emotional part of you;

o   Was that decision a wise one?

o   Was that decision thought out?

o   Were their consequences to that decision?

o   Do you remember how it played out?

Also take on board that at this time the **'reward centre'** of the brain is highly sensitive and a lot more reactive at this time, hence the impulsive risks that are taken in the teen years.

Add into the mix that the teens' peers play a vital role in how they define themselves and how they are perceived, so you clearly have a fire, firelighters, petrol and fireworks all in the same enclosed space.

We then expect our teen to think rationally and come up with a sensible decision! Is this achievable?

At this stage unless we have taken time to regularly sit down and talk through scenarios or read out stories of other teens situations, unless we have shared what consequences look like and or reiterated what rewards can be gained from wise choices, our teen does not stand a chance.

At this point our teen, unless they have been consciously coached to know 'how to think and how to make critical choices', is in the firing line of their emotional brain and choices of teenage life and peers, and feels overwhelmingly so, that they have A LOT to lose.

There are many ways to think and it can be seen and felt within our everyday lives and daily interactions. We can recognise that some people think in similar ways and others we have no idea how they process thought patterns. It is up to us as parents to be aware of how differing thoughts patterns impact on our teens' life.

The most important part is how the teens make sense of their thinking and how they have come to that place, the type of explanations they give themselves, as this is what impacts their emotional and mental health - our attributional style – 'Psychologists have determined three important types of attributional style;

*How personally we take events.

(Do we tend to blame ourselves for every set back rather than consider other reasons? Is it always our thought no matter what actually happens?)

*How pervasive we view events to be. (if we lose a job, do we think our whole life is ruined or do we view the damage as limited to a short period of time and consider the possibility that other career opportunities may open up.)

*How permanent we think an event is.

(Do we think a set-back will be short lived or go on forever?)

Human Givens, Joe Griffin and Ivan Tyrrell
www.humangivens.com
The Human Givens Approach

We teach our kids how to think from the minute they are born. We too have been taught this way, so unless we have taken time to reflect and make changes, we will be continuing previous generations' way of thinking, without actually knowing why we think in such a way.

Notice how it is that your teen reacts to life's situations, there are conversations to be had with regards to changing their processes:

o How does that way of thinking support you?

o   How do you feel about all of this?
o   Are there any other ways this situation could work out?
o   Do you know all that you are thinking is the truth?
o   What would help this situation look and feel different?
o   Is there anything you can learn for you about you & life from this time?
o   Can you recognise any habits in how you deal with situations?
o   How could you do this differently?
o   Who else thinks like this? What would you be saying to them?

Critical thinking is a skill and one that enhances how we look at different situations and then that in turn allows us different choices, empowers us. What a skill to give a teen who is living from their most emotional brain…

Create the habit of asking your teens questions that get them to understand, critically think through, the situation, to work out differing impacts, consequences and rewards.

• How are these things going to play out?
• What do you think that person was thinking?
• What could have been the consequences?
• What are the potential risks involved?
• How will doing this help, support or benefit you?
• If you were that person what would you do?
• Why do you think I want you to do this, help me understand?
• If this does happen what do you think is likely to happen next time?
• How will this help you achieve your goal?
• What is possible in this situation?

- What are the other options?
- Why do you feel this is best for you?'

If we coach our teen to ask themselves questions that allow them space to think through choices and consequences, we are building in the resources to 'think', creating the Neural pathways even though the brains structure is not in place.

We are creating learned behaviour to support the teen to 'think' well, developing the teens' brains to work to the best of their ability.

Add to the above questions;
Who?
What?
Where?
When?
Why? And
How?

What wires together, fires together!

What we repetitively do and how we think becomes a habit and structural within our brain. It becomes part of the neural structure, so coaching our kids to think through, around and differently gives them more choices, options and the confidence to believe in themselves.

'Whether you think that you can, or that you can't you are usually right.'
Henry Ford

When the teen has the habit of awareness of how they think, it can be extra supportive (especially at times when they are being influenced by peers to act 'impulsively') to have structures in place. We as parents must create another level of support and self-belief for the teen, along with the confidence to do what feels right for them as opposed to following the crowd.

A lot of thought is linked into emotional situations, it is our way of finding a way through something that feels uncomfortable, awkward or just unknown. We are very rarely taught just to feel, so we use our thoughts to try and control our feelings and, in turn, our thoughts are shaped by the very feeling we are trying to escape.

What if we allowed ourselves to 'feel' that feeling rather than trying to think it?

If you look at a beautiful picture or a sunset, you can see and feel it, but no words will ever describe it or create the same feelings that the image or situation created. Feelings have to be felt as no words or understanding will heal them. Thinking may make 'sense' of them, which is a comfort and way of dealing with the feelings, but it won't allow you to heal. Maybe if we teach our teens the power of their emotions and thoughts and how these two are independent of each other, not interdependent, then they can appreciate the power of, and in, feelings!

Emotions

A state of feeling, a complex state of feeling that results in physical and psychological changes that influence thought and behaviour.

Emotion is often intertwined with mood, temperament, personality, disposition and motivation. Our emotions play a massive role in our lives they add the 'third dimension' to our world, both enhancing and challenging us. It is for us to understand, feel and allow them to be so we can use them to grow through any situation. It is for us to have an emotional awareness and understanding of how we are who we are, so we are able to harness our feelings.

As a teen they are acting and feeling from the 'emotional part' of their brain as the logical part is in still in development, so we as the parent have a powerful role to play in showing the teen;

* how to behave when feeling emotional
* how to honour their feelings and working through them
* in reflecting with the teen after the event to gain insight into skills to support them
* in exploring tools and support systems so the teen can begin to learn more about how to feel
* in understanding our emotions and their development
* in finding ways through situations that are mutually supportive
* being aware of our emotional triggers as well as our teens
* the differences we share emotionally and allowing both
* in coaching them through times of high emotions in way that allows them
* in teaching them and ourselves emotional resilience
* in naming the emotions and the sensations that accompany them
* in engaging with and responding to as opposed to reacting and acting out
* learning to integrate feelings with skills to 'pause' and make choices
* learning the skill of observing the emotional self and integrating emotional and rational with engagement

The teen feels life and their emotions much more heightened than we as adults do, as they don't have the brain development, the scaffolding, to think or process differently.

When we fully understand this and work from this place, it allows us as the parent a more insightful awareness as to how to deal with the emotions of our teen. It teaches us to PAUSE and to allow for the reality of the situation for ourselves and for our teenager.

- What would support you when emotions run high?
- What would you like to do differently?
- What triggers you to feel emotional, overwhelmed, stressed?
- How do you self -care when life feels too much?
- How are you, role modelling emotions to your teen?
- What do you need to support you support your teen?
- How were you taught to 'feel'?
- Does your family have a culture of sharing feelings?
- How would you like to 'feel' different?

Many people do not even have an emotional language to describe their feelings as many cultures, until more recently have valued I.Q, intelligence quota, over emotional intelligence, EQ. It is only in the last 20/30 years that EQ has been recognised.

Emotional intelligence allows people to make better decisions, create a better quality of life, create a better standard of living through having and maintaining good relationships. EQ recognises, values and creates happiness and that is one, if not the one thing that all human beings crave. Being emotionally aware creates a different quality, texture to our life and those around us.

How can we teach our teens to live better lives, be happier and content to know and feel wellbeing?

Coaching them to feel, to know emotional intelligence to the same standard we school them. We have been taught that it is vital for our kids to have qualifications in order that they get a good job and live well, but at no point have we created a culture where to be happy is of importance. So many people have great jobs, earn money and yet happiness may allude them.

What is emotional literacy?

The ability to understand your emotions, the ability

to listen to others and empathise with their emotions and the ability to express emotions.

Coaching our teens to express and manage their emotions and respond to the emotions of others in ways that are helpful to them and others. The practice of interacting with others in a way that builds understanding of their own and others' emotions, then using this understanding to inform our actions.

We have all experienced disappointment, hurt, being let down, rejected and numerous other feelings that are uncomfortable. How we manage these can determine how we navigate a path through our life, if we can feel and learn from each situation then they serve to help us grow and become more through each experience. Life and our emotions support our teen to grow, if we have the awareness and understanding to 'feel' and heal.......

We have understood that the teen brain works predominantly from a place of emotions and at this point of their life they start to experience new feelings and situations, so it is our role to help support them to grow through these. Otherwise, we have a teen who begins to fear all that has hurt them. We have a teen who can feel anxious and overwhelmed by the hurdles of life.

Our emotions play many different roles in our life, so it is for us to teach them how to use them to support themselves. We have teachers for our teens to guide them through exams and academics, what about creating coaches to help support them learn to 'feel' and harness their feelings to enhance them!

There are so many feelings and yet so many of us have so few words to describe how we are feeling, so here are just a few:

Sad, lonely, vulnerable, despair, guilty, hurt, down, isolated, abandoned, victimized, fragile, powerless, ashamed, remorseful, empty, inferior, disappointed, angry, humiliated, bitter, mad, aggressive, frustrated, distant, critical, judgmental, withdrawn, annoyed, numb, violated, provoked, hostile, furious, dismissive, resentful, betrayed, fearful, anxious, insecure, rejected, threatened, nervous, exposed, insignificant, inferior, inadequate,

45

overwhelmed, frightened, scared, excluded, helpless, happy, playful, joyful, content trusting, optimistic, powerful, accepted, interested, free, cheeky, confident, creative, loving, thankful, intimate, hopeful, inspired, intimate.

Before we can guide our teens through this layer of development, it is a good idea to understand where you are with your emotional development;

- When did you last explore or understand your feelings?
- What do you do to support yourself emotionally?
- Who do you share your feelings with? Do you have a support network?
- Do you feel at ease talking about your feelings?
- How were you taught to 'feel?'
- How have you bought your teen up with regards to their feelings?
- When do you make time to check in with your teen emotionally?
- Who else can your teen turn to?
- Where do you feel most emotionally supported?
- How would you like to 'feel' differently?
- What do you think you could do to change emotionally?
- What do you believe about 'feelings'?

When you reflect back on your life, think about the numerous times when you were 'emotionally' hurt, when your feelings affected how life was for you:

- What could have made a difference for you?
- How would you change how you managed this time?
- How were you supported?
- What made this time different for you?
- What did you learn about life and yourself?

It is during our teenage years that our brains are working from their most emotional part and it is at this time that teens experience many emotional firsts, whether that be, love, loss, change, divorce or separation. These all require extra layers of support and emotional guidance.

We play the most consistent role in their life so let us also guide them through these developmental and emotional storms that can appear at this time.

There are no specific rules as to how to think and feel, however in order to make life easier for our teen helping them to see how they think and how this affects them might allow them the space to recognise there are many ways to think. If at the same time we can witness how they feel and support them, we can honour their emotions and help them create emotional wellbeing. We role model how they develop, so it really is up to us to coach them through in the most compassionate and supportive way we are able to, and at the same time we can learn more about our own emotional journey and what we need to develop further. It is also very important to give our teens permission to share and show their feelings and perhaps sometimes to not even know why they are feeling the way they are.

Tears don't have words they are their own language

Many people are denied the right to 'cry' as it can feel uncomfortable for those around them so the phrases, 'boys don't cry', 'tears won't help' and 'cry baby' mean that so many are taught to feel is not OK and to feel is not acceptable or safe.

Teaching our teen, the power of their feelings, the language of their emotions, the choices and responsibilities that are theirs, allows them to be able to draw boundaries and have a level of awareness as to how to deal with themselves and to manage the people around them.

Information allows us to be informed and with this the

teen can then be able to override the lack of structure in their brain and put in place habits that support them in everyday life and in building relationships and learning about the power of relationships!

It has been discovered most recently through neuroscience that our brain has the ability to adapt and change with all that we learn. Our brain grows and changes as we learn more, adapt and change.

We are therefore able to allow our parenting to form the underlying structure, the foundation, as and when necessary we become the scaffolding to support them when life feels overwhelming. We allow them to create their own systems of understanding, self regulation and management by holding a safe space for them to feel seen and heard.

Space for notes:

Mental Health

Mental health is 'the state of your brain and how it is working' how it feels, thinks, perceives the world and process' life and all that is happening around and within us.

You know that physical health is how your body feels so if you have a headache or hurt your ankle, you become aware of the feelings, the pain you are experiencing. In order to stay physically healthy, it is important, you eat, sleep, hydrate and exercise and to feel the benefits of good health.

Mental health is more complex and has been a lot less undervalued and we are less educated about it, for many different reasons. Mental health and mental illness until the last 10-15 years was very much taboo and unspoken about. There was a stigma attached to being mentally ill, whether this was fear, ignorance or a combination of the two, but it has been a dangerously well-hidden and dark secret.

However, we need to be as aware of our mental health as we are our physical.

We need to know what we are thinking and how that affects how we are feeling, as there are more mental health issues around now than ever before and it is affecting our teens in so many different ways. We all have mental health like we all have physical health, and it is learning how to understand what this means and how best to support this, for both ourselves and our teens.

Mental health problems often start in teens, and it is easy to dismiss symptoms as 'teen behaviour'. However, the sooner we can become aware of what is happening, the sooner our teen can get support. In order to know what mental health issues are, we also need to know what mentally healthy is. Finding our 'healthy normal' and then we are able to know when we are out of balance!

Some stats to highlight the mental health crisis that is taking place in the UK at present:

- 16 million people in the UK experience a mental illness
- 3 in 4 mental illnesses start in childhood
- 10% of children between 5-16 have a diagnosable mental illness
- 75% of kids are not receiving treatment
- 10 years is the average wait for effective treatment in kids
- Suicide is a leading cause of death in young people
- 18 people a day die of suicide in the UK

Mentally healthy then, is to be able to think clearly and rationally and on the whole to be mentally calm and at ease.

This in itself is a challenge for the teen, as it is at this time in their lives their brain is not fully formed, and they are living from the most emotional part of their brain. It is then our job to ensure that we are able to be aware of how they are dealing with life, friendships, social media. We need to know how they are thinking about themselves and their challenges in their emotional lives. This is a matter of 'checking in.'

How a teen feels affects how they think and how a teen thinks deeply impacts how they feel!

Think back to a time when someone had upset you, where does your thinking go and how do you distort the situation through your thinking?

In order to be able to support our teen, we need to be aware of where their head is at and what they are thinking, hence the importance of connection. Many parents don't want to interfere or are too busy…. It is VITAL that we have an understanding of the challenges and the changes that our teen experiences and how they process and deal with these.

Social media plays a massive role in our teens life and it has been seen through research that it plays a massive role in mental health issues.

Teens being 'digital natives' live a large part of their lives and social connections through their phones. Things are said, posted and shared that in reality, face to face may never be communicated. You know how it is to get cross in the car, or at the television screen and what you might say, scream or shout but in everyday life face to face would never utter the same sentiments! Screens are addictive and numbing making the teens world very distorted, with filters, lies and half-truths, it creates an environment, that is both competitive and insecure, as well as addictive. The impact: insecurity, fear, lack of confidence, toxic comparison and shallow connections that can be disconnected in a second. Social media plays a massive role in mental health issues, especially anxiety and depression. Many clients, I have worked with have learnt how to self -harm and even techniques to end a life through technology. It is all too easily accessible.

We have a massive responsibility as to how we let screens into our world, and where we create boundaries.

Let's look at the mental health issues that more commonly arise in the teen and then let's explore questions as to how we can be aware of how they are feeling and thinking mentally:

Depression

An illness where there are many symptoms:

Feeling extremely low, hopeless, futile in life, feeling tired, empty, overwhelmed, lost, suicidal thoughts, feeling disconnected, drowning internally, having an empty mind, loss of interest, no energy, oversleeping or not being able to sleep, feeling incredibly emotional, tearful or extremely angry, waking up tired, over-dreaming, having too vivid dreams, not bothering to eat, drinking too much to cope, losing perspective on things, feel like a burden!

Depression is horrendous, it strips the teen of all self-belief, they can easily be consumed by escaping the pain and this can create other issues, such as drinking and taking drugs.

Many teens I have worked with were too worried about what

people might think to share how they felt or when they had done people had said to them, "what have you got to be down about?" so they then questioned whether it was really an issue. That in itself dismisses the teen and it now becomes that it feels like there is nowhere to go. It is such a difficult time, it can also be scary to acknowledge for both teen and parent, however the sooner the mental health issue is acknowledged the sooner the recovery and support can be put in place!

What to do:

Talk openly, research what it means to feel 'depressed'.

Ask questions, reach into where your teen is and ask what they need to support them.

Be as open as you can and allow them the openness to share freely without making it about you or that they are scared to share, and of you are not able to talk find someone they can talk to, family member, coach, therapist.

Provide a space for them to share how they are.

Where to go:

Look up local therapists and ask around.

Find support groups.

Go to the Doctor.

Be open talk to friends, someone will be able to shine a light.

Look up mental health charities: MIND, REThink mental health, Samaritans...

How to deal with it:

Be open, talk, share, allow your teen to feel you have their back and you are in their corner, talking allows them to feel that they are not isolated.

Information:

Depression Alliance
www.depressionalliance.org
0845 123 23 20

Mind
www.mind.org
info@mind.org
0300 123 3393

Mindfull
www.mindfull.org

YoungMinds
www.youngminds.org.uk
ymenquiries@youngminds.org.uk
parents@yongminds.org.uk
0808 802 5544

Get connected
www.getconnected.org.uk
0808 808 4994
Text: 80849
Free telephone that connects young people to any and every helpline available

Youthhealthtalk!
www.youthhealthtalk.org

Youth2Youth (Y2Y)
www.youth2youth.co.uk
020 8896 3675
UK's first national helpline run by youths for youths.

Anxiety

Feeling scared, intensely worried and overwhelmed by life, fearful of life all of the time, where simplest issue can spiral out of control. Overthinking becomes normal and you get stuck in your thoughts, unaware that it is the anxiety taking over. Anxiety can also present as feeling unconfident, finding social situations too much, not trusting yourself, decision making becoming more difficult.

Symptoms are shortness of breath, shaking, sweating, feelings of dread, headaches, crying, tense body, unable to sleep, overthinking, and on occasions nightmares.

During anxiety the brain is in survival mode. The response is instinctive, primal and powerful, more powerful than any rational thought process and logic.

Anxiety has become all too common with 'teens' and perhaps some of this is due to technology and the intense pressure to 'be' whatever it is that is important to that teen. The lifestyle has a lot of teens on alert all of the time connected to outside of themselves.

When kids/teens get anxious they all too often act it out, so notice their behaviour, they may be more reactive, angry or closed down.

Research shows that social media for all its positives is also incredibly demanding, consuming and plays a massive role in how teens feel about themselves. 24/7 they are aware of who is doing what, where, with whom, what they are missing out on and what they were not invited to, and at the same time they get to see everyone else having 'staged' fun. Imagine that at a time when your brain is only working from the 'emotional' structure, so there is limited rational thought but overwhelming feelings of: perhaps, not enough, why not me? Loneliness, abandoned, take a moment to feel that sadness and confusion that may impact and overwhelm our teen.

OCD / Obsessive compulsive disorder

Obsessional thoughts and behaviours accompany **the severe anxiety**. These thoughts and images are obsessional and impulsive, unwanted, inappropriate and regularly very scary, telling the person a range of thoughts that will impact them. The anxiety is felt through not being able to control their thoughts, mind and the content that is within.

The compulsive behaviours are repetitive, and can be mental activity, to repeat certain phrases or numbers and the behaviours can be so demanding that getting out of bed in the morning can take so much longer as each ritual has to be acted out.

It is a very limiting illness and one where the person can be so trapped by their head and the thoughts that life becomes too hard. Many adolescents with OCD believe that if they don't do a certain behaviour something bad will happen to them or their family, so in their mind they are preventing a huge tragedy and therefore they feel that they really have no choice but to act out the compulsions.

OCD usually begins in adolescence. With the right support and treatment, it can be initially managed and then healed.

General Anxiety disorder /Panic Disorder

This is very different from ordinary anxiety as this is more severe and can impact on everyday life making everything challenging. It is estimated that 1 in 6 will suffer from anxiety disorder at some point in their life.

Due to the high levels of anxiety it is very common that panic becomes part of daily life.

With GAD there are physical effects that range from chest palpitations to dizziness through to muscle aches and pains along with stomach issues. Psychological side effects that impact every area of thinking; not trusting your mind, thoughts, decisions, overwhelmed by racing thoughts, restlessness, feeling on edge to repetitive and disturbing thoughts. These both impact on everyday life and the ability to manage, to cope.

Become more aware of what is happening for your teen and notice if they seem unusually 'stressed' by everyday life!

Some of the signs of this prior to it escalating are:

Inability to make everyday decisions
Overthinking every area of life
Continually needing to be reassured
Feeling stuck and overwhelmed by life

What to do:

Talk about it, ask questions, try to understand even if you can't appreciate it, put yourself in their shoes.

Do research and explore what is happening, teenage brain etc.

Show your teen your concern for where they are & again don't make it about you... they are scared, stuck and lost and need empathy, connection and guidance, you are their satellite navigation

Where to go:

Online is always a great bet, you can find any amount of information, so go searching, explore, books, tools and ways through.

How to deal with:

Create a calm base, home.

Slow life down and explore what is needed to make your teen feel safe – anxiety is when they don't feel safe in themselves or life, so it is up to the parent to put the scaffolding in place to create the 'safety' or the illusion of it.

Ask them to share their thoughts about what the anxiety is telling them and don't challenge just reach in and guide them through.

Know that the teen is trapped within the anxiety and needs skills to lower the intensity.

Information:

Anxiety UK
www.anxiety.org.uk
0844 775 774

No Panic
www.nopanic.org.uk
0808 138 8889

OCD action
www.ocdaction.org.uk
0845 390 6232
support@ocdaction.org.uk

OCD-UK
www.ocduk.org
www.ocduk.org/pdf/youngpeople.pdf
www.ocduk.org/pdf/children.pdf
www.ocduk.org/pdf/ParentsOCDGuide.pdf

CBT Online
www.getselfhelp.co.uk

Eating disorders (EDS)

The teenage years are a time 'bodies' become very important and food can become a very difficult issue. Eating disorders usually start as a teenager so the sooner they can be recognised, they can be managed, and support put in place. An eating disorder is when food becomes an issue whether it is to eat too much and binge or to deny food and starve, both of these if not caught earlier enough can become a lifelong torture. As a parent we role model our relationship with food and as a mother to me, it is vital that I teach my teens the power of their body and the healthiest relationship with food.

One in 10 people will experience partial or full symptoms of an eating disorder!
Royal College of Psychiatrists 2012

Body Dysmorphic Disorder

BDD is a type of anxiety related to body image, the person does not see themselves as they are, they see themselves as looking much bigger. They only see exaggerated negative and this becomes overwhelming and controls how they feel about themselves and life. Everyone gets down on themselves sometimes, but this becomes consuming and negative thoughts take over this can lead to depression and anxiety as life becomes too uncomfortable.

Binge Eating Disorder

This is the most common eating disorder, where the main characteristics are a preoccupation with body shape and weight, self-worth is dependent on shape and weight, regular eating habits of over-eating until incredibly uncomfortable in your body.

Bulimia nervosa

The most common eating disorder where the person binge eats and feels a complete loss of control and then self induces vomiting or taking laxatives to rid themselves of the food they have binged on. This becomes the cycle of life until treatment is sort. The signs that may allow you to recognise, is the person may go to the loo after mealtimes and or large amounts of food can go missing regularly. Again, like all of the mental health issues the sooner this is talked about and help is obtained the sooner a resolution can be found. As soon as you have a concern, deal with the situation, get your teen help; they are trapped in a cycle of living that is too powerful for them to escape and as far as they feel, they get something from it, the quicker the help the sooner the recovery.

Anorexia

This illness is all about control and avoiding eating, weight loss and starvation. It is common amongst teen girls as it can allow them an element of control when everything else feel out of control, when their body is changing, when the pressure increases, when they are beginning to become more 'feminine'... Weight loss is the main symptom, alongside loss of interest in food, avoiding mealtimes.

Teens may have an unrealistic view of themselves, seeing themselves as fat and having a very distorted body image. This can lead to obsessive exercising, cutting out certain foods, analysing calorie/fat content.

What to do:

Talk, be open, ask the uncomfortable questions.

Research to find out more of symptoms, characteristics, information

Feel the fear and do it anyway

Reach out to friends for support

Get professional help for you so you can support your teen

Make the uncomfortable, comfortable.

Where to go:

Doctor

Online

Local support groups

How to deal with it:

Don't make it personal, this is not about you or done to you, this is them out of balance

Gather all information, so you feel informed.

Have a rough idea of what you want to do to support your teen.

Put boundaries in place.

Get professional help as soon as you can.

Create recovery, support network for you and for your teen.

Know you WILL get through this and you can all learn from and within it…

Information:

Beat (Beating Eating Disorder)
www.b-eat.co.uk
help@b-eat.co.uk
0845 6341414

Anorexia and Bulimia Care (ABC)
www.anorexiabulmiacare.org.uk

Boy Anorexia
www.boyanorexia.com
Men get eating Disorders Too
www.mengetedstoo.co.uk

Self -harm

The clearest indication to look out for is the physical signs.

Self-harm is a behaviour and not an illness, it is a coping mechanism to manage the feelings of distress. Self-harm to the person doing it, feels like a way of releasing the pent-up overwhelming feelings that have no other way out. The person can go into a trance when they are harming, it becomes as addictive, or unconscious as say smoking is to a smoker!

Self-harm usually starts in the teen years:

13% of teens have tried to self -harm
Over 200,000 cases of self-harm are seen at hospitals.
1 in 10 young people have self -harmed
1 in 4 teenage girls have self -harmed
28% young women and 10% young men have self-harmed

There are many ways to self-harm from cutting to taking risks through to poisoning. Teenagers use self-harm as a way of releasing the build of up of emotions. It becomes a private ritual where they find some relief from the pain they are feeling. It is the only way they feel comfortable to manage all that is happening with in them.

What to do:

One of the most important things you can do as a parent is to ask what you can do to support your teen and then listen.

It is a scary time for you to see and know that your teen is feeling this out of control, however that is how it looks to you, to them they are actually in control.

LISTEN, PAUSE, SUPPORT, find a way through that allows them to know there is no judgement and there are other ways to explore their emotions.

They will not want to give this habit up easily, it is like their childhood comfort blanket or favourite toy, it creates an element of safety in an emotionally chaotic time, it is also addictive and there go to.

Where to go:

To your teen and ask them and let them become comfortable, through time, in sharing what it is, what it does and what it means to them

How to deal with:

Self -harm is challenging as no one wants to watch or know that their child wants to hurt themselves, it goes against our parenting skills, however, if we want our teen to trust us we have to let them lead us, put boundaries and talking in place but let them lead us through this time so it is at their pace and for them to find the necessary comfort and safety.

Panic, fear, guilt and shaming do nothing but disconnect everyone.

Get support in place for you so you are able to manage your feelings.

Information:

National self-harm network
www.nshn.co.uk
support@nshn.co.uk
0800 622 6000

Harmless
www.harmless.co.uk

Self harm – Young Minds
www.youngminds.org.uk

Mind Mental Health
www.mind.org.uk

Suicidal feelings thoughts….

Suicide is not chosen; it happens when pain exceeds resources for coping with pain.

Many people who experience mental health issues, many teens whose brain stops being a part of them that they can trust, see suicide as a way out of the mental pain. They see it as one of the only options to find relief, escape as life feels too much, the pain of living too overwhelming.

One of the **symptoms** of depression is suicidal thoughts, so not only is the teen feeling lost, low, hopeless, lethargic and disconnected they are also having thoughts of what is the point, thoughts telling them to kill themselves being the only perceived way out

Most teens feel too scared to tell anyone that they feel suicidal, that they have planned how they might kill themselves, because of others' reactions. As parents we need to be aware of what our teens are looking up online, too many sites act as 'how-to' guides with regards to suicide. We are the first line of prevention, so boundaries are vital and so is being curious as to their usage of social media. Let us build a community where our kids feel more supported.

Some, anti-depressants and medications used for teens can actually increase the severity of the suicidal thoughts, so be very aware that medication may have a place, but it can also have horrendous side effects.

So many people with differing mental health issues 'feel suicidal' as opposed to just having the thoughts. It is anxiety and depression that create the thoughts of not wanting to be alive, feeling like there is no air and each breath is too hard to take. It is a grey area as life can be ok and the suicidal feeling can still be there, so to someone not suffering or who has never had the thoughts it can be very difficult to understand. Maybe it is not for us to understand but to HEAR what is being said and appreciate the teen is **scared** of their own mind, imagine that!

Please know for the teen it is both a very scary place to be, and on occasions the thought of not having to deal with life with a mental health issue can mean it is also a relief.

There are also different types of suicidal thoughts. Passive suicidal ideation is to not want to be alive but to have no plans to kill yourself, and active suicidal ideation is to have the intent and the plans to do it. The more information you have the more you are able to support your teen and get the right help.

Having worked with thousands of teens, many of whom have had the thoughts and strong urges, but none have taken their lives, I believe because they have a place to talk about the feelings, the thoughts and when they share them there is an element of dilution. The thoughts are still there but they are not just trapped within their heads and the pressures eases slightly. It is making the scary, less scary. It is lessening the appeal of 'relief', it is attempting to explain that this is transient, it will pass and there are brighter days ahead even if they can't be seen at present. It is the tunnel metaphor, there is always a point within a tunnel when you are mid- way when no light can be seen, that is the space of suicidal thoughts…. That darkness!

- Every day 2 people in the UK under 24 kill themselves
- For those aged 15-24 suicide is the second most common cause of death
- A conservative estimate is that 19,000 cases of attempted suicide of teens, each year that is one every 30 minutes.

What to do:

TALK, TALK, TALK!

LISTEN non-judgementally

When a teen knows that suicide can be spoken about that their thoughts have a place, it allows them to feel supported and it can alleviate the pressure of the thoughts…it becomes safe to talk about something that feels both scary and relieving.

Be receptive without being judgemental

If you make the first move to talk, be gentle and don't use guilt or why would you do this to me?

It is NEVER personal to you but to them, to how they feel and what is going on within them!

Your teen may feel great shame and confusion at having these thoughts so the braver and more loving you can be as a parent the more they can begin to feel 'safe'.

You are their safety net.

Also please do not buy into 'if someone talks about suicide, they are not going to try to act it out.'

Where to go:

Reach out for help, speak to the Doctor, find support groups, help your teen to get their support group- people they feel safe talking to.

Information:

Samaritans – 24-hour help line specialising in emotional support and trained in listening to people talking about suicide, desperation and despair
0845 790 9090
116 123
jo@samaritans.org

Stamp out suicide
www.stampoutsuicide.org.uk

PAPYRUS (Parents Associations for the Prevention of Young Suicide)
www.papyrus-uk.org

Mind
www.mind.org.uk
0300 123 3393

ASIST (Applied Suicide Intervention Skills Training)
www.livingoworks.net

CALM (Campaign Against Living Miserably)
www.thecalmzone.net
0800 585858

Mindfull
www.mindfull.org

The Mix - a free support service for under 25s
0808 808 4994
help@themix.org.uk

Rethink Mental illness
www.rethink.org
0300 500 927

Mental health issues can be incredibly frightening and scary for all involved. It can make everyone feel unsafe, as no-one knows how best to deal with the given situation. As a parent you can feel powerless to be able to help, to create a quick fix. It is also a highly emotional time as everyone is living in a place of 'unknowns' and fear, so get support, talk, share and do not let shame or embarrassment prevent you getting all that you need to find resolutions.

From my years of working with teens and emotional and mental health, the families I have seen that manage it the best for everyone involved – do these things:

1. Talk and create an environment that is safe for the teen to be open
2. Parents recognise they too need support
3. Not take it personally
4. Not try to find blame as to why this is happening- find support and make a plan
5. Use it as learning curve that your teen needs more and is acting, thinking it out
6. Be open to learning about the condition or illness and how it feels
7. Compassion and Empathy go a LONG way on this journey
8. Be open

9. Do NOT make it about you, if you can't cope get extra help
10. Understand just how HARD this is for your teen
11. Create a CALM home and help your teen by understanding them
12. LISTEN, LISTEN, LISTEN
13. Step back where necessary and be led as well as lead
14. Believe that you will get through this and be honest about what you need
15. Create new habits, routines and get as much scaffolding in place to support everyone.

Signs of imbalance, knowing what mental health looks like

A healthy teen, like all human beings, will experience mood swings, tiredness, ranges of emotions, worries, overthinking, overeating or undereating, sleeping too much or too little, these are just part of the roller coaster of life. The signs of mental health issues are when the teen feels that a factor impacts their life in such a way that they find it difficult to maintain a healthy balance in life.

When they stay in their room more than they connect with people, friends and family, when even the simplest task becomes challenging, when they appear to sleep a lot, have minimal motivation, overthink even the most basic situation, stop or dread doing things that they enjoy, they withdraw from their own life. Before it becomes incredibly apparent that they are struggling check it out with them, reach out and ask them how life is. Some parents are too worried about upsetting their teen that they let the situation roll and this is when it can become serious, when intervention then takes longer, as the mental illness mindset and habits have set in.

A lot of mental health issues in teens can be prevented by talking or educating ourselves as to how to best support our teen. It is interesting how most parents are happy to get a tutor for their teen, or extra sports coaching, pay for a pair of trainers or computer game, but therapy or coaching can feel difficult or uncomfortable.

However, in today's world, and with the interconnectedness of life, our teens need to have support in many different ways as their world is more and differently demanding than that which we have known.

How do we ask our teen how they are feeling and thinking, mentally?

- Tell me what's happening for you today?
- How do you feel?
- You seem low, is everything ok?
- If 10 is good, happy & calm where are you today?
- How are you going to create calm today?
- What's the plan for your weekend?
- What can I do to support you right now?
- You seem to have stopped doing the things that make you happy, any reason for that?
- How's your thinking?
- Are you sleeping ok?"

There are some really simple basics that we have to ensure our teen puts in place EVERYDAY, otherwise they do have massive impacts on their mental health, mood swings:

1. Enough sleep, neuroscientists say 9 hours is optimal, so perhaps 7-9 hours.
2. Decent nutritious food that create sustainable energy.
3. Physical exercise everyday if only a walk to and from somewhere.
4. Connection, to take time to be with people.

5. Boundaries for screen time.
6. Awareness as to how they feel so maybe a scale, so they become aware of mood changes.

If we help support our teen to create a list of basic needs to live healthily, we are enabling them to create the scaffolding they need. As and when life is challenging, and it will be, they will have an understanding, of what they need to support themselves.

As a parent, our mental health is vital, and it is our responsibility to ensure that we look after ourselves and all that is needed to support our health. If we choose not to share these issues with our children, it may well be that they 'feel' it and act it out in other ways.

Many of the teens that I have worked with that have anxiety have a parent that suffers with anxiety, and some of the behaviour is learned behaviour. If we want to support our teens to find a healthy balance with their mental health, we have to role model what that looks like.

With regards to parental mental and emotional health it is no surprise that the teens that have parents who are more open to share how they feel and are more open to talk, have teens that are more open to talk. There are so many situations in life that we as parents go through and if we recognised that emotional upheaval, trauma and upset we have opportunities to teach our teens that there are many different strategies and ways through situations, whether that be loss, grief, divorce, illness or any other life changing issue.

How we view life is how they view life, how we deal with life is how they learn to deal. So perhaps notice if your teen is struggling with mental or emotional health issues where might they have learnt this reaction, behaviour.

Some mental health issues start as an emotional situation that is ignored and then becomes too much to handle, and instead of it being 'feeling based' it becomes 'thinking based' so it has now taken over all of how our teen is; their mind, body and feelings!

Space for notes:

Mental and Emotional health continuum

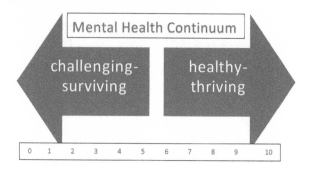

We all live within a mental and emotional health continuum, so when we talk about mental health it applies to us whether we have suffered with an illness or not. Let's explore what this might look like, and it will be different for all of us but here is my understanding from the work I have explored...

SPECTRUM:

> 0
>
> What is the point in life? Feeling hopeless or overwhelmed where life is either too much or not enough. Cannot cope with feelings and wanting to find a way out. Thoughts overtaking and destructive to continuing life. Thinking is out of control and life feeling too painful. Suicidal?

> 1
>
> Feeling like losing control of mind, thoughts, feelings and cannot see a way out. Life is becoming too hard, each breath difficult. Feels too hard to share and don't want to burden others, so keep drowning in the thought...anxiety, depression, sinking inside.

TURBULENT / UNSTABLE

2

Mind consumed by unhealthy, unhelpful thoughts, cannot find a balance, need a space to talk to share but too difficult to reach out. Know this place and feels like drowning within yourself. Disconnection from self, empty, lost, dark, scared.

3

Noticing mind is either racing and overwhelming or lost and dark and empty, powerless to change. Not present, losing connection to self, emptying, triggered by so many different areas of life. Life not easy anywhere, no more pretending, energy hard to find.

DESTABILISING

4

Overthinking, stressing, body showing me how I feel. Mood changing. Aware of changes more difficult to make but know that if help there can choose to do this differently, fight, flight or freeze...

5

OK – neither good nor bad, not really present, just being a "human doing." Doing life but not feeling anything either way.

6

Mind is able to find clearer, cluttered as well, like seeing light at end of the tunnel but still in the tunnel. Want to see different ways through, want to make different choices. Stuck (ish) but awareness of paths in front. Having the right support to make choices. Feeling more space within, elements of calmer... there are pauses between the thoughts and feelings.

STABILISING

7

Aware of thoughts and thinking, see, hear and know there are choices, maybe not clarity but like the fog is lifting, everything beginning to tick along, some semblance of normal.

STABILITY

8

A new clarity, thoughts are by choice, feelings are uplifting, there is space that you both choose and is there, feeling calm, a base of ease, and able to see and feel choices. There is a point to life, and you have purpose and direction.

9

All is well, life feels good. Thinking is calm, mind working in balance and sees the future and all the opportunities, choices and you are able to trust the process of life.

10

CONTENT. EASE. HAPPY. LIFE IS A GIFT. A MAGICAL PLACE TO BE.

GRATITUDE. CALM. BLISS.

We will all experience elements on this mental health continuum, it is for us to be aware of what our mind, our thoughts are and to be able to notice how we are feeling.

By understanding our mind and our thoughts we can then support ourselves and our teens to put all that is needed in place, whether that is to find calm, or whether that is to seek help.

Mental health is vital to how we live our life, we all understand what physical health means now it is time to fully understand the value, importance and the level of priority mental health care needs to play in our and our teens life.

If we don't think well, we don't live well; invest time and understanding in your mental health. There is no health without mental health.

Space for notes:

Emotional Wealth

Emotions are the weather in our internal world. To feel allows us to recognise all that is going on within. However, if we are feeling overwhelmed our thinking isn't too clear. Emotions can be the storm in our life, and it can feel like everything is raining down. Our feelings greatly impact our life, which, in turn, affects thought processes and patterns.

Emotional wealth is to be aware of the power of feelings and to be able to recognise how we are feeling and to sit with those feelings. It is our job to teach our 'teens' that their feelings add to life and the more that they can embrace, feel, sit with and allow these feelings to come and go, noticing what is going on for and with them, the greater their emotional understanding or 'wealth' will become. Just like adjusting our clothing depending upon the seasons, so to we need to acknowledge and adjust to allow for our feelings and thoughts to change and evolve.

Too many people have been brought up to ignore their feelings or to translate feelings into thoughts and then somehow expect these thoughts to deal with and heal the feelings. Imagine seeing the most beautiful sunset, your eyes sense the beauty, your mind appreciates the magic, but no matter how you try to describe it, no words will do it justice. Just as this is the case, so too will no words take away sadness, or pain, you will, understand the reason for the sadness, but no thinking will heal the feelings.

We need to be more aware to support our teen as the most emotional part of the brain is managing their life, their world is being steered by their feelings and the teen hasn't been empowered as to the gift of their emotions.

In order to make life simpler it is so important to teach our teen to check in with themselves:

o   How am I feeling?
o   How is this affecting me?

o   Who can I share this with?
o   What do I need to accept this?
o   Is there anything I can do to feel more at ease in this?
o   Is there anyone I know who can help, support me?
o   How is this impacting my life?
o   What allows me to manage this time differently?
o   Reminding them this will pass...

Once the teen is made aware of the power of their emotions and can acknowledge them; for example accepting they are in a bad mood because of tiredness, it is for us to accept that this is not the time to start reviewing life, as they will do it in negative self-talk way. Instead, find a time where both you and your teen are in the right headspace to discuss emotions in a positive way.

Let us educate our teen to know what it is they need to:

Acknowledge their feelings
Accept their feelings
Not act on their feelings, immediately
Share their feelings
Sit with their feelings. PAUSE
Support themselves

We are creating a teen who is able to recognise the power of their emotions, to feel them, to grow through them and able to self-regulate and therefore stabilise themselves, to allow themselves to grow through the difficult times, the challenges of life, to become emotionally resilient and at the same time to immerse themselves in the power of the positive feelings.

We are giving the teen the ultimate gift, the presence to feel their life every step of the way.

Take time to explore:

When someone ignores me, I feel....
When someone cries, I feel....
When someone praises me, I feel....
When someone talks about me, I feel....
When someone gets angry with me, I feel....
When someone breaks my confidence, I feel....
When someone is attracted to me, I feel....
When someone criticises me I feel....
When someone is late, I feel....
When I am new to something, I feel...
When someone deeply understands me, I feel...
When someone listens to me, I feel....
When someone disagrees with me, I feel....
When someone gives me an order, I feel....
When someone puts me down, I feel....
When someone shows me love, I feel....
When someone gives me a gift, I feel....
When someone makes time for me, I feel....
The feelings I find difficult to express are....
The feelings I find easy to share are....
The feelings I have more often than others are....
The feelings I rarely have are....
The feelings I worry about are....
The feelings I keep to myself are....
The feelings I want to be able to share are....
The feelings I grew up with in my childhood are....
The feelings I share most with my kids are...

The power of emotional wealth, the currency to 'feel' life!

you can't hide from your feelings
thinking them doesn't heal them
try leaning into them
try sitting with them
try making friends with them
be kind to yourself
be loving with yourself
& as you feel
you HEAL

life.

Space for notes:

Chapter 3

THE ECOSYSTEM OF RELATIONSHIPS, SELF, FAMILY AND BEYOND

Moods & Mindset

"**O**ur teens need us to stand still and hold the ground steady for them. If we push against them, we make it easy for them to pull away. If we pull away, they will feel the void where the love, support and connection should be."

Karen Young, Hey Sigmund (Facebook Page)

A mood is an emotional state.

In contrast to emotions & feelings, moods are less specific and less intense. Moods are internal states that affect the persons behaviour and interactions. Adolescence is a time of mood swings and it is important that we are aware and able to respond more than we react to these moods. It will also help us if we can become more aware of our 'moods', as again learned behaviour will play a role in how our teen acts out their moods.

Take time to notice:

★ What and how are you when you are in one of your 'moods'?

★ Where did you learn to manage your moods? And have you?

★ Allow yourself to witness, without taking it personally; How does your teen act out?

★ How do they react?

★ What are the similarities?

★ What do they need at this time? Do you know?

★ How can you support them to recognise their 'moods'?

★ Are you able to communicate with them & how they feel?

★ What will allow you all to navigate this time without it becoming overwhelming?

★ What do you need to allow you to stand still and hold the ground steady?

Due to the power of the teen brain and how it is active from the most emotional region, it makes sense then that the teen's moods will become more heightened and they can become more reactive, as they are living from their emotions, their feelings. Intense emotion can lead to moodiness. Being aware of this is not an excuse for your teen to be moody but it is for you to allow and accept that they do not have the same brain structure that you do, so they are actually designed to feel more. We are the more experienced ones so we do have more responsibility to respond to the 'mood' not react.

Moods swings are a very normal part of the teen years however it is also a time when mood swings can impact mental health and if not monitored can lead to mental health issues.

Being aware and inquisitive as to how your teen feels is vital in order to monitor if they are struggling with their moods, or if their thoughts are becoming overwhelming.

With major mood disorders it is not usually just one thing that affects and impacts the teens life, you may find; friendships, schooling, sleep and or eating can all change, which is why your daily awareness of your teen plays a role in supporting them as and when a mood becomes more than just 'moodiness.'

- How do you feel?
- What happens to you when your mood changes?
- What are you thinking?
- Does it feel difficult to become calm?
- What can I do to support you? How can I help you?

I have explored earlier some of the signs of mental health and the way forward when health is affected mentally. So many times, the 'teen' doesn't want to burden anyone or is understandably scared to discuss how they are feeling. It is therefore so important that we as parents have the understanding, awareness and insight to be able to support the teen at times that they feel exceptionally vulnerable.

Mental health issues **CAN** occur during teen years, in fact 50% of all adult mental health issues started in the teen years, which is why being aware and educated can mean we can get the help as early as possible to support the journey to recovery.

Mood scale & awareness

Being aware, conscious of our moods provides insights as to how we or our teen are feeling and what is happening within that time that impacts us and our lives.

CALM is the healthiest place to be and it is necessary for you to be in this place as often as possible as it acts as a mood anchor. If you can take yourself back to calm then you will REBALANCE quickly. If you are living in anxiety you will usually drop into depression, as to live with high energy and negative thought is unsustainable, so creating calm and calming habits will support you to find and live with more stable moods. Mood stability is a vital tool in life, to be able to recognise how you feel, where your mood is and find a way back to stable and calm. Calm is the place we need to create more of in our teens' life, teaching them what their calm looks and feels like.

MOODSCALE

How do you feel? 10 is your best mood/feeling!	Description of mood. How do you feel?	What makes you feel better? Next step up
10		
9		
8		
7		
6		
5		
4		
3		
2		
1		
0		

This tool allows for you and or your teen to be aware of their moods, feelings and what supports you or them to move through their moods. When I do this with clients, I will start by saying: "recall your happiest, calmest best mood or feeling ever and describe it to me"– this then becomes the number 10- and then start to explore "okay, so what is your worst feeling, mood", for some it is lost, lonely, others it is anxious and panicky, every one of us will have different moods and or feelings for each number. Once you have plotted the feelings, moods then it is time to explore what would allow you to move towards 10, explore who, what, when, when, and different activities that create a change in their mood!

Like a see saw there is a tipping point, it really helpful to recognise where, when and what this is. **As parents we role model moods!**

Many of my clients parents complain that their teen 'worries' a lot and can overthink a situation, so I ask the parent a few questions and it can be seen that the parent has unknowingly taught their teen the art of overthinking, so it is now a team solution to get parent and teen to 'notice their thinking' 'to watch their mood.'

When working with clients who have big mood swings; the first step is to mood map to understand and see how the moods impact, so creating an awareness then to notice the moods, not judge notice then to become aware of any triggers – was it in reaction to a situation, lack of food, sleep.

Once you have the insights then you can make a plan to change the behaviour:

What would you like to do instead of over-think?

How would you like to manage that situation next time?

If you could go back and speak to that you, what would you tell them?

How to recognise your mood to support you?

Alongside your teen, acknowledge how you feel, what is going on and how you can best firstly sit with the feelings to recognise them and then what will allow you to heal and grow through them. Sitting with feelings, which is what can underpin our moods, gives us the choice in accepting all that is going on. Our feelings are our satellite navigation, they let us know experience a deeper quality of life. The mood scale is a tool that allows your teen to become conscious of where they are with how they feel, because their brain is led by the emotional part, their reactions, moods and thoughts can be extra sensitive. Making moods more conscious gives the teen the tools to support themselves, along with the awareness. This allows for the development of the neural structure, which is not yet fully formed, to create a habit, a positive learned behaviour. You have bypassed the 'lack' of control and created a learned behavior, putting the correct structure in place – you have built stable scaffolding. With awareness and differing skills, you can respond to external situations that impact your mood and you can find ways to deal with your mood, so that you manage it and do not react! **You** get to choose. **You** have created the power to choose how to respond.

Many of us are taught to numb out, ignore our feelings and when we do, we numb out all feelings, the challenging and the good. The mood scale enables us to recognise, name and feel everything and create tools to support us and our teen.

Space for notes:

Becoming & Un-becoming, learning what no longer works for us!

Who are you?
Who am I?

The teenage years are the first real major time in how teens define who they are: their dress sense, their beliefs, their friendships, their choices at school, how they spend their time, their hobbies, their understanding of their role within the many differing roles that they play in life. All of these choices are gradual and evolving, so it is not that teens make daily conscious decisions, it is that over time they are influenced by peers, the media, music, differing role models and they pick and choose how they want to be, where they want to fit, or not, what is important to them, what risks to take, what boundaries to break, who to listen to, who to be influenced by.

At this point in the journey of your teens life your influence will have daily perhaps hourly changing impacts due to the changing feelings and emotional swings within the teens' world. It is therefore even more important that **CALM**, and practicing the **PAUSE**, is used as at this time the teens brain is highly reactive. So many times, the teens behaviour is in reaction to a power struggle to show you they are more 'independent' than you allow them to be. Getting the balance right is important. Knowing how you & your teen react, having consequences in place and guiding them through the powerful surge of feelings is helpful and sets up a base for them to practise when in times of conflict.

The growth into themselves is happening on so many levels, the teen is physically changing, their bodies' developing in many differing ways. The teen is having to find comfort in a body that does not feel like theirs, their height, weight, skin, voice, sexual organs are all undergoing major growth, they are being flooded with the sex hormones and this in turn is affecting both sexes in numerous differing ways. They are at the same time becoming sexually aware of themselves, their bodies, their feelings and what it is that interests and excites them. It is a whole new world of sexual awareness, one that is much more than anything our generation have ever known, more choices, more labels and so some might say more confusion!

We can teach them what we know and then let them teach us what they know...

Embrace the journey and the differences!

There are some conversations that can support this time to allow for the teen to find comfort within the acceptance and safety of the relationship of their parent, their primary carer:

How do you see yourself?
What words would you use to describe you?
Where do you feel most comfortable in your life?
Where do you feel most uncomfortable?
What feels most challenge right now?
Where do you feel most yourself & why?
How do we hinder your growth?
How do we support your growth?
What do you need from us to help you?
What do you learn from us? Despite us?
Where do you see yourself?
Do you need to fit in & if so where?
What do you think we are teaching you right now?
What are we teaching you?
What can I/we do to help you become more you?
How can I/we best support you?
Where do you find it easiest to express yourself?
How different are you with your friends?

What would surprise us about the you that you become outside of home?

As our teen develops, alongside their growing brain it is for us to provide the scaffolding, the boundaries, for us to recognise are we acting out of love? Compassion? Understanding? Or out of fear, hurt and from the wounds of our teenage years?

How we act teaches our teens' how to act.

The becoming of our teen is an incredibly powerful time of development and if we let it be, as we witness their changes, we can also take the time to look within and notice ourselves, how we came to be or how we can un-become what no longer fits with us! We always have choices in each and every situation. We have a choice in how we respond, feel and deal with it. We can choose to continue with the pattern set up in our childhood. We can notice new habits and ways of dealing and reacting to situations or we can become really conscious of our behaviour and create or imbed new ways of being.

There has been no greater time for self-awareness, self-development and change than now. We are becoming more aware of the brain, habits, psychology and the ever-changing world of one's 'self.'

Perhaps then some questions to support you as the parent of a teen:

What were your teenager years like?
If you could go back and write a letter to the teen you what would it say?
What would you like to have done differently in your teens?
What was life changing in your teens?
What helped you through your teen years
What teenage beliefs still drive you?

What teen choices still affect, impact you?
What teenage events still impact you and your life?
What held you back?
What influences how you parent your teen?
What would you like to do differently now?
What can you begin to change?
How have you grown from that teen you?
What would your teen say about the teen you?
If you watched a movie of the teen you, how would you be feeling, what would you be thinking and saying?

We have all been teenagers and it has had life changing impacts on us in one way or another. Now we have the chance to walk with and lead our teen through these challenging, sometimes force eight turbulent times in a way that is both conscious and compassionate. If at the same time we can allow the teen to see our vulnerable side, we can give them permission to access that part of themselves.

As role models however, we act, behave and respond, no matter what, we are teaching our teen, how we expect them to be. Therefore, what and how we see our teen behaving can in some way or another come back to what we have shown and taught them in how to be.

Notice what it is that triggers you to react to your teen and notice your reaction, then perhaps take the time to look within, to reflect and become aware of how you are in comparison to how they are behaving and you will see what it is that is having the reaction in you!

If you were looking back at this stage in your parenting, what would you be choosing to do differently?

How can you parent more consciously?

What are you, role modelling with regards to 'becoming?'

What are you learning about you at this time?

At every stage throughout our life we are able to learn and grow, to keep a growth mindset, to be open, to step out of our comfort zone and to be open to our learning and growth zone.

Humility is the gift of keeping an open mind, to not think the we know everything, but to be aware of other perspectives and new ways to live, to be!

Our teen can be a guide in a different way that we are to them. It is entirely up to you as to whether you are able to step out of your comfort zone, through the fear zone and role model what the learning and growth zone looks and feels like!

Space for notes:

Acknowledgement and acceptance

To be loved, is to be seen for all that we are and still to be accepted, despite our behaviour, despite our opinions, despite our moods, our attitude, our habits. To be loving is to share this, even when our teen is pushing every button, acting out and challenging – to love is to be able to let the other person know I am here, in your corner and I have your back. "I see you & I believe in you".

I am obviously not saying that we accept all of our teens' behaviour, attitude and actions, but that we learn to look deeper into what they are doing and why, that we acknowledge their behaviour is not who they are but how they are acting out. We know that when they were toddlers' we expect tears and tantrums as they are learning, growing and frustrated by life, so as teens it is to be expected as they are experiencing life differently, they will be acting differently. When we are able to view behaviour as a sign of something more and not make it personal to us, or a reflection of who they are then we can become more understanding, more aware, more insightful and use the issues as sign posts to what is going on with our teen.

- Are you aware of all of your weakness' and strengths'?
- Do you acknowledge and accept yourself?
- What do you find difficult to accept about your teen?
- Where do you think are your blind spots?
- What parts of you don't you accept?
- What parts of you were you taught as a teen were not acceptable?
- How have you learnt to befriend those parts of you?

What is it that we all as humans crave?

There are some very basic human needs, that humans require

to thrive and to feel loved and accepted is one of the most basic. However, we all feel and know love differently:

- What makes you feel loved?
- What makes you feel abandoned, rejected?
- When and who do you feel acknowledged by? How?
- Do you know what makes you teen feel seen? Accepted?

To be accepted and loved for all that we are, is a gift and one that empowers us to feel more at home in how we are and who we are!

Perhaps in order to acknowledge and accept our teen we can take the time to more fully understand and accept ourselves.

Changes and Consistency in unstable times

'The only thing that is constant is change', Heraclitus

The teenage years, as we have discovered both in our everyday lives and within the pages of this book, are a time of great changes and instability. The brain, the major organ within us that guides and controls our lives and the motherboard to living, is for the teen going through the most powerful and life changing developments. It is being pruned so that it is more effective and efficient and, thus, is not fully formed, therefore the teen is living from the most emotional part. Living through these times is a bit like having no brakes and using the gears of our car to stop us, a different way to drive. It is then for us to have a whole new level of understanding and appreciation of the importance of **calm**, **stability**, **response** and **gentleness**, so that while the teens brain is going through the most massive 'brainstorm' we are able to anchor them.

A force 8 gale only impacts and damages the boats that aren't securely anchored!

How do we anchor our teens during these precarious times?

The biggest changes are invisible to the outside world, all we see is the actions, behaviour and attitudes that come from the changes, so perhaps our role is to:

- Strong boundaries- do what we say we will in all areas and stick to it.
- Calm communication -speak clearly and often as to feelings expectations and create understanding of all the instability.
- Be the port in the storm -allow the teen to know you are there when they need you & you are their biggest supporter, actions and words.
- Be consistent- when they are emotional and overwhelmed, don't meet them when they are, be calm.
- Don't take the behaviour personally- they are not acting out to piss you off, they are sharing how they feel through their actions, in therapy it is called communication by impact – they let you feel how they are by what they make you feel.
- We anchor ourselves daily, hourly, minutely if necessary and we PAUSE, PAUSE and then PAUSE again, counting to 10, 100, 1000 whatever it takes to lead them through the challenges of their most turbulent times.
- We remind ourselves, our gorgeous teen does not have the 'mental' equipment needed to anchor themselves and we DO, so we are the adult... it is a great time to learn a whole new level of patience, tolerance, acceptance and unconditional love

Our teen is expected to navigate their way through some big decisions. The teen is expected to study hard, to get good grades, to maintain and create new friendships. During this time, they may see parents go through hard times, may lose people or pets they love for the first time. The teen will be challenged as to what they believe in, will be tempted to try new legal and illegal experiences, may fall in love, lust and at the same time fall out of love and lust, all whilst their brain is undergoing monumental changes. Their bodies are developing and may be feeling alien along with the surge of hormones and chemicals urging them to take risks, as well as being overwhelmed by new desires. And we wonder why our gorgeous teen may struggle?

Our job then is to be the **CALM**, to create, share and teach **CALM**.

Being calm, take a moment to pause, allows us to find compassion and any situation becomes manageable and resolved in a healthy way, teaching your teen that there is always a way through.

Space for notes:

Death, Divorce, Distance – major life changes

As the adults, the parents, we make decisions on a daily basis that have an impact on our teens' emotional wellbeing. We decide what the best information is for them to become aware of, we decide what we think they will be able to manage, but do we ever stop and think about the impact? Short, medium and long term. Do we ever ask: So what is it that would help you manage this situation better?

We can never know exactly how our 'teen' will feel and deal with situations, but if we don't talk to them, if we don't support them, if we don't allow for them to have a rich open and honest emotional life, then we hinder their development, healing and growth.

I have worked with so many teens that have been 'shielded', 'protected' and kept 'safe' from situations that are unravelling around them, only for that protection to come back and cause more pain than the situation itself. The biggest and probably hardest experiences that 'teens' need guiding through are difficult and often painful situations, all that they need to be shown is how to 'feel and grow' through some of the biggest changes of their life to date:

- Serious illness of a family member
- Death of someone known
- Separation and Divorce
- Family changes, new partner – blending families
- A parent moving away &/or playing emotional games
- Friendships and the complications
- Relationships, first love & all that entails
- New beginnings
- Uncertainty and change

Is it then our job to know that our teen will travel through many uncomfortable and awkward situations and it is for us to talk, support, guide, role model and have the courage to be there, to ask the difficult questions, to own our emotions, to be present even when every fibre in our body wants to distract and minimise the situation, feelings, the enormity of whatever it maybe. It is to find the balance between honesty, courage and guidance. It is only through experience that we learn how to find our way through the challenges!

- What overwhelmed you as a teen?
- Do you remember how your parents dealt with change for you?
- How do you feel about change and loss?
- How have you led your children through big life events so far?
- What do you need to make it easier to be more present?
- How difficult do you find talking emotions with your children?
- Is it difficult for you for your 'teens' to be overwhelmed by some life situations?
- Do you feel confident in guiding your teen?
- Are there people in your teen's life you can steer them towards to support them?
- Do you 'over protect?'
- Do you overshare?
- Do you share the truth, elements of what is going on?
- Are you able to reach out and ask others for ways through?
- Do you take into consideration the differing impacts of the situations?
- How can you begin to manage change mentally and emotionally?
- What are the differing lessons to be learnt from the experiences?

There are so many different life experiences that our teen might grow through and we cannot plan and think out what they might be! We can deal, feel look, explore and learn what each one may allow our teen to feel, realise, learn and grow through as they, we go through...

- The power of emotions and emotional wellbeing
- Feelings and the importance of acknowledging
- Resilience
- Communication and sharing how we feel
- Responding to others not reacting
- Learning to reach out, ask for help
- Courage to feel
- Change and the impact

The illness and death of a loved one is very common in the teenage years. Different people deal with this in differing ways and usually it is to protect the teen, which is fully understandable. However, how will they learn about loss, sadness, grief and managing the pain of change unless we allow them? It is not emotional abandonment, rather a level of respect to allow them to feel it. Is it then up to us to be discerning with the truth and to allow the teen to play a role in their awareness as to loss, to grief and grieve?

When we overprotect, we disempower our teen to grow and we then make life more difficult, even though our intention was to make it easier!

How will we teach them to grow through if we don't let them go through the loss?

Role modelling, talking, sharing, asking questions, being open, sharing tears, feelings and stories allows the teen to know this is all normal to feel overwhelmed by loss.

Grow through what we go through.

I have worked with so many teens who have been through deaths of all different kinds, expected, sudden, tragic, suicide and many more and the teens who are able to process it better are the ones who are led through the pain, not the ones who are shielded. Many of the teens who are shielded then believe they need to protect their parents and it becomes a circle of unexpressed grief and pain that can result in the teens becoming emotionally and mentally out of balance.

The teen having been shown that it is scary to feel then gets scared to feel as they believe the feelings will be too much when in actual fact it is not feeling that becomes overwhelming, it is the bottled up feelings that then become anxiety, deep sadness and an overall confusing mix of unknown feelings that occur a while after the loss that don't seem to have any reason whatsoever, due to the fact a significant amount of time may have elapsed.

It is our job to teach our children that emotions and feelings are not be feared but embraced, felt, healed and grown through.

Space for notes:

Separation and Divorce

As an adult and partner in a relationship, we are aware of our relationship and its longevity, however our children did not choose to be in the relationship. They are a product of a once loving relationship, so it is again for us to be the adult and to guide them through the 'adult world' and its choices with respect and awareness as to the impact of the situation on them. Many adults in this situation, feeling overwhelmed, tend to get lost in their feelings and become less aware of their teen. You are role modelling relationships, you are teaching respect, change, decision making, growth, endings and if you are reacting then you are teaching your teen to react.

Responding is a much more powerful place to be, to know your feelings. To feel your feelings and then to take time to find the best way through them is to 'respond.' To react is to act within and from the overwhelming emotionally.

When families break up, when parents go their different ways it is incredibly difficult for everyone involved but as the 'child' they have had no role in any of the decision-making process and they are powerless to the changes that have been made. Understandably the adults are emotional, hurt and managing life and their feelings. Regardless of the adults' emotions, these questions must be asked of the teen:

- how and what is the teen learning?
- what is the impact on the teen?
- What have they learnt?
- What are they left feeling?
- How can you make it an easier transition?
- Have you asked your teen what they need?
- What do you need to make this time feel 'safer?'

A parent moves out of the family home, the dynamics of the

relationship change, the teen is left to deal with adult changes and that is life, they can often feel powerless.

Separation and divorce can have a catastrophic impact on our teen, the not knowing, the life changes, the pain of watching people you love hurt and sad, the distance of family, being in different places. The new way of living and then the back and forth of moving between homes, people and new environments.

As adults we make choices and I wonder if we talk about the truth of the feelings, of the reality of the situation!

One client I had worked with had lost a very special grandparent under very traumatic circumstances, the parents made a decision not to tell their daughter, the daughter found out and then lost trust in her parents. Her life felt bleak and she became very depressed. She acted out her anger on everyone, but especially herself, she self-harmed in so many ways, became destructive to the point of suicide attempts, never succeeding, but the pain of loss, of grief was acted out as opposed to have been felt.

The parents did what they thought was right, their daughter needed more information, support and time, she needed others to know she was hurting, and it was overwhelming. Through therapy this teenager has become the most incredible advocate for mental health and her courage is inspiring. All she really needed was permission to feel, to grieve and to be angry that the world has snatched her favourite and most trusted person from her.

As a parent we lead our teens as we have been led, unless we have made choices to be different. Our parents were of the generation of 'war surviving' parents, times are so very different, we are no longer living in the state of survival. It is the time to address our mental and emotional life so VERY differently, really understanding what it is that our teen needs especially in times of turbulence and instability!

We have choices to grow through what we go through and make it our job to both role model and teach this.

Space for notes:

Chapter 4

HOW TO BE YOU (WITH THEM), IT CUTS BOTH WAYS

Personality types and the impact

A type of personality defines the way a person can be characterised by their preference of attitude. It can be a challenge when you have more than one child and the children are all so very different. However, the primary challenge is to **NOT** compare...

Many parents assume that their child will be similar to them and treat them accordingly, the child grows up with the similar lifestyle, values, beliefs and attitudes but the difference is in the personality, the part of you that underpins all of the behaviours. As a parent one of my biggest learning curves was that my son was highly sensitive and intuitive, I knew nothing about these traits, so I have learned and tried to understand where and how life feels for him and in doing so have become more authentically me as I realise parts of myself that were not previously recognised.

As a parent our reflection of our child, allows them to know themselves If we are forever telling our child, 'they are not good enough' they will learn they are not enough – our perception of

102

them and what it means to parent them initially defines how they are who they are.

Carl Jung defined the personality types into 4 different preferences, this was in 1971. This has since been developed further and is insightful into understanding how your 'teen' views the world and it is a great tool to have to understand the differences between you and your teen.

The preferences

Extroverted / Introverted

This is the sense of the persons energetic expression. An extrovert will feel energised by being around others, they feel more alive in company and get their energy externally.

An introvert gets their energy from within and has a rich internal world. Today's world is geared towards the extrovert; fast paced, socialising, sharing on social media platforms and the ability to connect 24/7. An introvert needs to decompress from the everyday speed of life, from people and too many connections, this 24/7 culture can be too draining.

If we are able to have an awareness of which of these our teen might be, and it is usually a mix of both, then we are able to parent them in according to what they need as opposed to what we need.

The second criterion is Sensing / Intuition

This is the method as to how someone perceives information.

A person who senses mainly picks up information from the external world.

Intuition is to gather information from the internal world or imagination, from within, based on what they feel they should do.

The third criterion is Thinking / Feeling

This represents how someone processes information. Thinking is therefore mainly through the mental process, working it out through thoughts.

Feeling is where someone chooses their emotions as an indicator

The fourth criterion is Judging / Perceiving

This reflects how a person implements the information they have processed. Judging means that a person organises life events and sticks to a plan that is more rigid and strict.

Perceiving is to be more adaptable and spontaneous, able to improvise.

Personality is just one element of our teen that guides their behaviour and it is also the part of us, the parent, that may create friction which then impacts the family dynamics and in turn how the family works.

It can therefore be very powerful to understand how each personality interacts and what would support healthy relationships.

When we as the parent recognise the differences between us and our children, we then have a choice as to how to manage the relationships. Many teens feel like they don't fit into their family as so much is changing within and this plays into how they relate. We can take what we know about our teen and we can use it to support what they need to make the healthy connections to allow them to feel like they fit within themselves and due to that within more environments. The teens are not meant to be mini versions of us, they are their own person and it is for us to recognise, acknowledge, honour and celebrate this, not try to control them to be versions of us!

In order to understand the differences that can divide

relationships and communication, take the time to know yourself and how you interact within the world:

What is your personality type?

What drives you to be you?

What do you need to feel safe? Thrive?

How do you communicate?

Do you love socialising?

Do you need time alone?

Do you crave company?

The best way to understand more fully the differing personalities within your family is to take a test:

www.16personalities.com

www.icould.com/buzz

Space for notes:

Self-aware, self-care, self-love = Self-worth!

So many years of education and no one taught us how to love ourselves and why it is so important!

Self-awareness is the key to emotional intelligence; to know oneself and have a clear perception of our beliefs, attitudes, strengths, weaknesses, traits, emotions and motivations. It allows us an understanding of ourselves which in turn supports us in having awareness of being mentally and emotionally present in life as it unfolds, supporting us to manage people and situations in a way that enhances our development and thereby gives us the power to respond and grow through life as opposed to react and shut down. When we are aware of ourselves, we have the power to make better choices as to how, who, where and when best supports us. It is not always an easy journey becoming more self-aware, to look within and feel the emotional and mental wounds of life and to take time to heal them.

If we as parents are prepared to do this work, we then become the best people and role model this to our teens. We show them it is not always easy to 'feel' life - in fact sometimes it is deeply uncomfortable, awkward, difficult and challenging - but it is authentic, liberating and allows for a better, deeper and more loving self-care along with more honest and real relationships.

Every relationship we have is based on and from the one we have with ourselves, so the most important connections are reflections of our relationship with our self. All that your teen is showing back to you are the parts of you that you have neglected or that are conflicted internally!

- What do you think of you?
- 5 words to describe you?
- What do you love, like dislike about you?
- What changes have you made to support you as a person?
- What changes have you made to support you as a parent?

- How have you grown with your teen?
- What are your strengths?
- What are your weakness'?
- What beliefs support you, work against you?
- Are you open minded?
- Where in your life are you most self-aware?
- What would people say are your blind spots?
- How often do you react to situations? What triggers this?
- What do you & your teens argue about most?
- Biggest conflicts in your home? Life? Self?
- If you could heal elements of you what would they be?
- If you could upgrade yourself mentally and emotionally what would that be?
- What does self-aware look and feel like to you?
- Which aspects of your relationship with you do you recognise with your teen?
- What part of your teen still plays out within your relationships?
- How would you want your relationship with your teen to be different?
- What skills would support and enhance your parent/teen relationship?

To value ourselves is self-worth, to know what we have learned and decide are our conditions of worth. Your childhood, parenting, family, teachers and friends will all have played a role in how you value yourself. We learn by how people treat us. What we are not aware of is that at the point of learning the people around us can only treat us in relation to their self-worth, so if we grew up with a parent who had tough or emotionally neglectful childhood then they cannot loves us more than they have either learnt to. In understanding our self-worth, we have to be aware of our conditions of worth so complete the following sentence, any thoughts or feelings that link into this.

If I am to be of value I must…

Maybe ask yourself:
How did you learn this?
Do you have memories linked to this?
How has this condition of worth impacted your life?
Are there any conditions that you have made linked to your condition of worth?

Self-care

A vital component for a healthy life is self-care. Self-care is a necessity in all aspects of yourself, physically, mentally, emotionally. In order to be able to live well, we have to ensure that we have all that we need so that we function from the best possible place.

Physical self-care – feel body well

- Sleep well and enough hours
- Eat well and nutritiously
- Hydrate – drink enough water
- Exercise daily
- Relax and rest
- Take supplements or medication where necessary

Mental self-care – think well

- Create calm time
- Limit worry time
- Be aware of your moods and manage and support them
- Notice when you are triggered by life, people and situations

- Practise mindfulness, being present – stops worry taking over
- Learn techniques to support mental calm
- Notice thoughts that don't support you and create ways to think well

Emotional self-care – feel well

- Take time to know how you feel before it overwhelms you
- Know what, who, where and when brings you back to balance
- Know what, who, where and when takes you out of balance
- Put calm, slow time in diary
- Make time for a healthy social life
- Share how you feel
- Journal if sharing is difficult
- Take time out for you every day if only 10-20 minutes
- Feel life and give yourself permission to feel everything
- Create playlists that support different moods
- Know what you need when life feels too much

Self-care is intending, planning and actually taking the time to attend to your basic needs.

Many parents do all that is needed for, with and to their children, neglecting themselves and then wonder why their teens might be extra thoughtless or selfish. You have role modelled that your needs don't matter, as you have neglected you, you have taught them to neglect you.

If you want a well-rounded, thoughtful, kind, self-aware and self-caring teen, guess what? You have to be that for, and with, yourself. To let them see and know that self-care starts with SELF! It is not selfish. It is like looking after a car and giving it fuel, checking tyre pressures, oil, and water. It is necessary for it to run well, as is self-care for you!

A lot of parents I talk to give their kids everything they never had, but their teen never missed it because they have you, so you still neglect you, as you are giving what you never had away but not to yourself. This is your chance to change that, to recognize your needs and to make changes that support your growth and healing.

You can over-compensate with your children and then neglect you. What you have created is imbalanced relationships, where your teen has their needs met at a cost to you and that in itself is the relationship, they can grow to expect from all around them!

You have role modelled to them to meet others' needs before they look after themselves and that others will take care of them, but they don't have too...

Self-love

How can we teach our teen to love themselves, when the world around them is teaching them that they need to look, act, feel, wear and be a certain way to fit in, to be accepted, to be enough? When the virtual world is teaching them their self -worth and self- love is dependent on how many likes they have, how many followers; a world where the value and opinions has become more important that themselves! A world connected more by screens than feelings, more by likes than words, more by selfies than sights, more by competition than co-operation, more by knives than kindness!

We teach self-love by loving ourselves as much as we are able at each step of the journey.

We teach self-love by not comparing ourselves, by accepting ourselves even in the darkest times.

We role model self-love by being as loving as is possible.

It sounds so easy and yet life takes over and the first thing that we forget can be ourselves, our needs and our balance, so we then role model "I am my last priority!" Sometimes the easiest way to self-love is to add small things to your life, to tweak what you are already doing to make it easier.

The question we can ask ourselves each morning is:

What is the most loving thing I can do for me today?

Only you will know the answer to that, it may be as simple as getting up 10 minutes earlier, so the school run becomes easier, it might be to eat breakfast or take a lunch break, it might be to share how you feel…. If every day started with that question, maybe each day would feel more loving.

Take time to think about some of the loving things you could do that would enhance your day, week and month and then plan them, add them to your diary and commit to doing them as you do to ensuring your teen gets to their activities.

A happier parent makes for a happier teen and in turn an easier and happier life for all involved.

We all ensure that our car has diesel, petrol, water and air in the tyres so then it is safe to drive, however we are not as aware of what we need to ensure that we make our journey through life as well fuelled and we are as healthy.

When we fly we are told by the staff, as part of the safety guidelines, that if in the event of air masks being needed we are to ensure that we put ours on first before we attend to others, as this allows us to support others more efficiently and effectively – well life is no different, if we don't attend to our needs we are less able and capable to look after those around us.

Self-awareness then leads us into **self-care** and this to **self-love** and as can be seen these are all vital elements to well-being, mentally, physically and emotionally. They are necessary to live calm, well and happily.

How will life feel and look when your self-care is part of your daily routine?

Self-love then is the key ingredient to a happier, calmer and more fulfilling life; so if we are able to role model and teach this to our teen, we are giving them a life-long gift that enhances and shapes how they are who they are and every interaction they have starting with themselves. We are showing our teens your best friendship starts with you.

Space for notes:

Relating & Relationships, Connecting, Communication & Compassion

Every relationship we share and participate in starts with us, so whether it's our teen, our partner, parents or friends, how we relate to them starts with how we relate to ourselves.

Maybe take a moment and reflect on your relationships:

- What do you find difficult within your relationships?
- What triggers you?
- What annoys you?
- How easy are your friendships?
- Do you trust people?
- Do you give easily?
- Do you receive easily?
- Are you forgiving and accepting?
- Are you approachable?
- What would the 3 closest people say about you?
- How would you describe your relationship with your teen?
- How would they describe their relationship with you?
- What do you observe in your teen's relationships?

When you become more aware of how you relate to yourself and then others, you may start to see where your teen has learnt to be like you or decided to not be like you!

Think of 3 or 4 people who influenced your relationship skills, who are these people and what message did they teach you?

Self-awareness starts when you explore how you got to be you. You will have unconsciously picked up your ways of relating from how your parents taught you & how they interacted with you.

Many people still carry and act from the wounds of their childhood and if we never look at and heal these, then we continue to act them out in many different ways, so a lot of relationships can start from a place of fear, hurt and vulnerability as opposed to love and acceptance!

- Do you want to change how you & your teen relate to one another?
- How do you want it to be different?
- What do you need to do to create the changes?
- How can you do this?
- What do you need to support yourself to create these new ways of being?

To be able to have healthy loving relationships with others, it is important we look at how we relate to ourselves.

If you are fearful, critical and judgemental of yourself you will be this within your relationships, if you are controlling and unforgiving with yourself then you too will act this out upon others and all of these traits and habits usually start with how you were parented, with how you were treated by your first and most important care givers, and they in turn by how they were treated.

This is not about blame, it is about accountability, it is about **becoming** more self-aware as to why the relationship with your teen is based on so many different factors some of which you are blind too and have more power than you realise. Therefore, becoming more consciously aware of ourselves, our behaviours and how we shape our relationships.

The quality of how we connect to others depends on how we connect to ourselves, it is very easy to be a people pleaser but actually not feel the pleasure of the people we spend time with.

Look within to see what it is you are role modelling to your teen about relationships, boundaries, giving and receiving, balance and kindness within friendships!

Friendships are what add too and enhance our lives and experiences, so without the right people around us, life can feel flat, empty, lonely and we can feel lost and disconnected. If friendships and relating to others is a basic human need, it is important to be aware of how we are who we are within these interactions.

Communication plays such a vital role in our relationships, it is how our teen knows what they mean to us, what we expect from them, what we are able to do with and for them. Communication guides us as to how we are and who we are and yet so many people are scared to communicate their truth for fear of upsetting others; when in actual fact, from all I have witnessed, it is what is not said or the tone in what is said in the parent teen relationship that has more impact than the words actually spoken. The voice, tone and words we use to communicate with our teen also then become the internal voice they communicate with themselves, so watch how you are with your teen, take time to observe your words, tone and methods of communication.

Having good communication skills is having the ability to be able to actively listen, to hear what is being said and what is being communicated through body language and tone. So many of the teens I work with want to share so much with their parents but are worried, it will upset, worry or be too much for the parent to hear, so they hide how they feel and end up feeling worse, alone, disconnected and can create unhealthy coping mechanisms.

To communicate well is to listen with an open mind, as well as being aware of your feelings as they arise, learning to manage them so you are able to **respond** to your teen not **react**.

It is important that there is time for you both/all to share, whether it is meal times, car journeys, walks or at the end of the day, but so many people have lives that are busy or are connected to their technology and then lose the time and space to share daily:

- Is there the time and space to talk?
- Are you approachable to talk too?

115

- Do you have to find a solution to the issue, or can you just listen?
- Do your emotions get in the way?
- Who does your teen share with? Do you know?
- Do you share openly if it feels appropriate?
- Do you come from a family where emotional chats were encouraged?
- How do you deal with issues when they come up?
- Are you able to listen actively?
- Do you feel heard? Supported?
- What could you do for you, so you are able to support your teen more?
- How would you feel if your teen shared, they were struggling emotionally/mentally?
- Do you have a strong network of friends, family to support you?
- How could you communicate better?

Teenagers can find talking to their parents or an adult incredibly awkward. However, once the teen knows they will be listened to and not judged, once they feel they are in a safe space then they have the support to be aware of all that is going within them and this allows them the space to witness their thoughts and start to make more informed choices, it allows them the clarity of mind to review all that is happening within and around them.

It may not be that talking is a strength, so in this incredibly fast paced world, conversations start via text, or it may be an email that allows the teen to share. It is not the medium that matters but the content they choose to share. I hear teens say I want to share this, but I am worried about the comeback or that the conversation will continue to repeat over the next few days and weeks, so is it that we learn what it is our teen needs to feel at ease to talk to us and then we learn and practice these skills.

I am not trying to say that we as parents are led by all of our children's needs, but I do want my teens to know that I am their biggest supporter, their most loyal fan. I would want the honour of being one of the places and people they feel safe enough to come to at all times, but especially when they feel lost, vulnerable, confused and emotional, as if it is not me, how will I know they are getting a loving, well-rounded understanding of their issues.

If we are the parent who raises their voice regularly, who reacts with over-spilling emotion, whose anger erupts first, who cannot hold their own feelings safely then we will not feel like a safe person to trust or turn too.

It is then our job if we want to create and maintain a healthy relationship with our teen to learn and understand what it is our teen needs to feel safe and at ease enough to talk about the 'stuff' that throws them.

I have worked with thousands of teens over the years and in turn had many conversations with their parents and so many of the parents are able to change and grow along with their teen and it is such a gift to witness relationships heal the wounds of both parent and child.

- How were you supported emotionally as a teen?
- Were your parents' people you would share with?
- What would you have like to have had as a teen?
- What did you learn about your feelings growing up?
- Do you share your feelings openly now?
- Do you trust people to support you through tough times?
- What could enhance you and your teen with regards to communication now?
- How do you react to emotional situations?
- How do you show how you feel?
- Can you be open with your sadness, pain, hurt and other feelings?
- Do you speak or act out your feelings?

Perhaps take the time to reflect on your emotional strengths and weakness' and allow yourself to explore further what it is that will support you to be more compassionate and loving both for yourself and then in turn for your teen!

Connection is the key to a good relationship, it starts with communication and understanding!

Space for notes:

Resistance and resilience

The teen years can be a time for our teen to resist what they have been brought up to know, they may be challenging the status quo because they can and because they are asserting their new-found level of 'interdependence'.

They are becoming themselves!

We expect our teen to step up and learn new skills, new ways to be, and to be able to start to navigate their world more independently. They have more freedom and more choices as well as increased expectations placed on them, and some-how we want them to do it our way because it has worked for us. We want them to continue our patterns, whether that be tidiness or organised or to be communicative or aware. What we fail to appreciate is how can they become themselves, unless they resist us? How can they know who they are unless they challenge who we are? If they do all we expect of them they become versions of us, not themselves. It is for us to guide and support them, it is for us to be shaped with them where appropriate and stand strong where boundaries are required.

Is it for us to close the bedroom door on chaos and appreciate the new dress sense?

Is it for us to recognise the power of and in resistance?

If we bring our teens up where 'our rules' are the only way to live then we create adults fearful of challenging others, that obey every rule just because.

Maybe it is to be very aware that our teen is acting from the most emotional part of their brain, so they will need guidance and help with many differing situations, but perhaps it is for us to support them as they find 'their' way through as they discover what works best for them and their understanding. Otherwise we are resisting who they are for the sake of who we are!

- Where do you & your teen meet resistance?
- How do you manage the situation?
- What challenges you about how your teen is?
- How do you resist change? Challenges? Life?
- What do you need to navigate the resistance?
- What understanding would support you more?
- How do you feel about being resisted?
- How were you bought up where rules were concerned?
- Can you not comply?
- Where would you like to bend with regards to your teens' needs?
- Where do your boundaries work for and against you?
- What changes would support your relationship?

We want our teen to be engaged in life with a good social circle and many activities all of which is going to have them interact with numerous different people. In turn we are going to watch them change because they are being influenced by a variety of people.

It is for us to learn how to acknowledge the 'sticking points' and learn to talk through resistance, to find ways to respect that working through allows for resolving and to find a resolution is a life enhancing skill!

To be able to meet someone where they are and understand the differing views and see all sides of a situation, means that everyone learns and grows despite the outcome!

Keeping an open mind allows you to see you all points of view and find a mutually supportive one.

Resilience

Resilience is a skill, an ability, mentally, emotionally and psychologically coping with a situation and managing it with a level of calm, to not feel overwhelmed by whatever it might be that is being dealt with. To find the courage, to go through the fear in whatever situation and to learn and grow whilst going through whatever life throws at you.

Resilience is therefore a necessary life skill that supports our teen to be able to manage life no matter what is thrown at them. It is a skill that is learnt only by experiencing the challenges of life, mentally, physically and emotionally. Our teen has to feel life, to explore life to be hurt, let down, upset, to fail, to not make the team, not get the invite, the award, the desired grade. If our teen never fails or experiences the more painful experiences and all the emotions that life has to offer then they will never need to learn to be resilient.

Many parents that I talk to will do anything to ensure their teen has all their needs met in every way possible. They are scared of their teen being upset by life. However, how do we teach resilience unless we know how to be resilient? The only way to become resilient is to go through the challenge of life and to be open to learning through them:

- How well do you deal with challenges in life?
- Do you grow through them or close down to them?
- Are you able to reach out for support?
- If 10 is most resilient where are you on the scale?
- What would allow you to manage the difficulties of life better?
- Where do you overcompensate with your teen?
- How can you support your teen to become more resilient?

Emotional resilience then is to go through situations that feel, uncomfortable, scary, awkward and unknown and to be able to access all that we feel and grow through, as opposed to shut down in the face of it. It is to have the courage to keep growing through life and through our emotions so that we learn from any and every situation we experience.

Many parents have learned from their parents, and their parents before them, that displaying emotions (to feel) is weak and scary. People can often be fearful of them and perhaps overwhelmed, so it is safer not to feel.

However, all this does is set up a default reaction to store the feelings rather than experience them, so that at some point we either don't feel anything or we get to a point in our life where every feeling we have ever had, like a volcano, erupts and flows in to our lives, our relationships and can have harmful impacts on our mental and emotional health.

Happiness is not achieved through being shut down.

As role models, is it our job to show our kids how to feel, how to drop in to their emotions, how to sit with sadness and grow through the hurt in their life, thereby allowing them also to recognise the magic in happiness, the gifts in calm and the growth through sadness. To sit with an emotion, is to take time to notice what you are feeling, where you are feeling, and to just be aware, embracing the tears, sadness, or whatever it is you are feeling, that way you dilute it. Many people try to think a feeling, but that is like trying to describe a sunset with words, no words will ever create the same image as the reality of it. No words will lessen the feeling. However, they can aid in analysing, making sense of them and rationalising them

To heal you have to feel!

Emotional resilience is having the courage to feel life, to embrace the differing emotions we feel and to become a better parent and person whilst teaching our teen the power of feeling! Resilience is knowing that no matter what life throws at us, we can learn from it and we can evolve through every situation to know ourselves better, to look at how we are who we are and determine what serves us and what does not. Resilience is a gift we create and allow ourselves as we ride the rocky roads of life

Space for notes:

Balance & Boundaries

Balance is a word that conjures the image of a tightrope walker as they focus on the journey from one side to the other. Life can be seen and felt as a balancing act and this can be witnessed especially in the teenage years, this is the initial time of exploring the big wide world more interdependently and how they navigate this is dependent on how they have been role modelled.

"Emotional balance' is the ability of mind and body to maintain an equilibrium and flexibility in the face of challenge and change. Emotional balance promotes physical health and is a prerequisite for personal wellbeing and growth. Many teenagers are allowed the freedom to roam the virtual, the gaming and the movie world highly unsupervised, watching and playing materials that are way beyond their mental and emotional age. This has been shown to have serious mental health impacts! However, they can then be confined to a controlled physical world where they are monitored and fussed over as a lot of parents see the world as a place to 'fear', a place where worst case living can become very normal and influence the teens confidence, self-belief and ease in navigating everyday experiences:

- how do we teach our kids to find balance within their mental, emotional and physical world?
- how do we allow them to grow and be challenged in different ways?
- how do we trust that we have instilled in them what they need to know in order to firstly 'survive' and then to 'thrive'?
- how do we teach interdependence and understanding?

As their role models we do exactly that, we portray to them what emotional balance looks like, we show them the truth of how life feels by continually talking, sharing and keeping an open dialogue as to how they are learning to 'become'. We allow them a healthy and age appropriate freedom to explore many different relationships and experiences all of which they can learn and develop through, we give them the choices in how they deal with situations whilst ensuring they know that they have our support and we have their backs when needed. So many parents will do all they can to safeguard and over protect their kids so they don't have to experience disappointment, sadness, and other feelings people judge as 'negative' but that then means we teach our kids that those feelings are 'bad' and we don't allow them to grow through them, the growth that will shape them to be an independent adult. We limit their experiences, so balance can never truly be found if you are not able to view all that can be felt, it becomes 'limited'. Like a bird in a cage the sky can be seen and not felt. Through limiting their experiences, we then close down the ability to grow, so the teens don't learn resilience, balance, or many other tools to find a way back to thriving. They lack the skills necessary on an emotional and mental level to grow through the experience and develop. It's a bit like learning the alphabet but only partially, learning from 'A' through to 'M' rather than 'Z'.

Creating and maintaining balance is a daily skill as we are affected by the world in so many ways, and in order to learn where our emotional and mental tipping points are, we need to be able to feel and notice those points. It is therefore vital to be aware of how the life we have led has impacted our mental and emotional world as well as ensuring we teach our kids/teens these skills. This can be done by checking in with yourself on a regular basis depending on how you are doing. If life is stressful, hard work or challenging, then checking in more often is vital, asking yourself:

How do I feel mentally?
How is my thinking at the moment?
How do I feel emotionally?

What is happening in my body, my feelings?
How do I feel physically?
Where am I holding my feelings?
How is my body feeling?

Balance is a daily act of awareness and creating emotional balance becomes part of your daily routine to allow for wellbeing

Boundaries

Personal boundaries are guidelines, rules or limits that a person or in this case a parent and teen create to identify reasonable, safe and permissible ways for other people to behave towards them and how they will respond when someone passes those limits.

They allow your teen to feel grounded and thrive. They are built out of a mix of conclusions, attitudes, beliefs, opinions, attitudes, past experiences and social learning. Personal boundaries help to define an individual; achieved through setting limits, physically, mentally, emotionally, sexually, materially and with regards to time. They operate in two directions giving both people the 'respect and safety' they require to operate in an environment that feels healthy and necessary for their wellbeing and growth. When we have healthy boundaries, we create healthy relationships. It is our role as the parent to teach and role model what these boundaries look like and that starts with how we behave.

All of our boundaries have been taught to us unconsciously through our parents parenting, so you may not even be aware of what yours look and feel like. Let us explore what yours look like so you in turn can be aware of what you are teaching.

It can often be seen that the disagreements that happen within the parent/teen relationship can be due to unknown confusing boundaries where there is the clash of two different boundaries, so if we understand what ours are, we can then explain the reasoning behind them.

- Are your boundaries like a brick wall or a door that can swing open or shut? Porous? Rigid? Healthy?
- Do you know why you have set the boundaries you have?
- Where your childhood boundaries reasonable? Have you changed yours in reaction or response to these?
- Have you considered why and how the boundaries you live by support you?
- Review your boundaries in the differing areas and relationships in your life, where are they the healthiest? Why?
- Have you explained to your teen the reasoning behind the boundary?
- Are you able to communicate and negotiate the boundaries?
- Which boundaries have you had for your pre- teen could do with reviewing for your teen – can you share responsibility for the boundary setting?
- What boundaries does your teen have? Are you aware of them? Do you respect them?
- How would it help your relationship if you & your teen sat down and talked through your differing boundaries and ideas?
- What are some of the actions you can take to improve your boundaries?

Setting boundaries for teens teaches them that they have responsibilities and actions have consequences. This allows them to understand that there are rules for living in society and the workplace. It sets them up to live well.

What are some of the boundaries that allow teens to know where they stand?

- **Bedtime, bedroom hygiene, privacy**

The teens bedroom is their 'space' a place where they are able to retreat into to be with themselves. It is important that we respect that this is maybe the only place that feels 'safe' so it is vital that as parents understand what that means to them. Knocking and waiting before you enter, not going through their private stuff, understanding they may not want to tidy every day and learning to be ok with that. Really getting the importance of respecting boundaries and the teens body and their room are the only two physical places that they are actually in control of. Bedtime is another really important boundary as sleep and the quality of sleep is a game changer, it impacts the teen in all areas of their life. Knowing what you expect and what works for your teen is so important, sleep allows resets in so many ways.

- **School attendance & homework**

Teaching your child routine and accountability comes in many different forms, attending school and supporting them doing their homework is just two ways. Many parents ask, push, cajole and then lose it where homework is concerned. How about talk? Support and then if the teen is still not working, step back and let them learn the consequences of their actions. In every situation there can be a learning curve for you & your teen!

- **The Body, food & exercise**

A teens body is a complicated relationship, one that they learn from the world around them, social media, friends, parents, tv – this initially starts with the parents and how a parent views their body, so a mother who diets will teach her daughter that either the body's intake needs to be strictly controlled or the exact opposite, as she has witnessed that control. A father who disrespects his body may be teaching his son not to care. It is for us to find a healthy balance with the body, food, and exercise. If we can learn about our relationship with our body and food and look at the beliefs that need working on, then we can role model to our kids, our bodies are in need of constant awareness and this relationship is vital to our health and happiness. Your body is your first home, treat it in a way where it feels good to live in. A very important part of the teens body is the massive changes it is going through on every level, the chemical, hormonal and physical growths can have the teen feeling like they do not feel comfortable being in this ever-changing environment. It is so important that we support and allow our teen to explore their feelings about their body, again asking some simple questions;

- What is the best thing about you physically?
- What is your body teaching you?
- Can you feel physically uncomfortable sometimes?
- When do you feel happiest with your body?
- Why would you compare yourself?
- Does comparing yourself support you?

We live in a society that has incredibly distorted views of what a good body looks like. A good body looks like one that feels healthy, active, energised and thriving again. We need to teach our kids, that surgery, injections and obsessions don't make you feel better, they hide the pain of not 'feeling enough'!

- **Mobile phones & screen times**

This is a highly sensitive subject and one that parent and teen will have disagreed about many times. However, it doesn't have to be an issue of conflict if the boundaries are adhered to and respected. We cannot as parents set rules and then blatantly break or not have similar standards for ourselves. You may decide to make certain rooms and times screen free, or maybe there is a specified time on a regular basis where everyone is screen free for a period. Screens are addictive in every form, so it is up to us to create RULES as to how we want them to be a healthy addition not create an ADDICTION.

With computer games again it is a conversation, negotiations and clear and well-defined boundaries. I have heard so many family rows start with "get off the game now!" and then all hell breaks loose; it is for us to understand the game needs to be played out until the end and the teen given consequences if they don't do as asked. Screen times can also be used as a reward, again allowing your teen to understand the give and take in relationships. We all need connection, human connection but the virtual world has a magnetic addiction that is breaking down all levels of personal connection and interaction and it is for us to remodel how that looks in today's world. It is for parent and teen to find their way to a healthier understanding and negotiations as to how this works and they may change but it is about mutual respect and understanding.

- **Chores**

We want our teens to help around the house, but if you have never asked them to do 'jobs' before, and for most of their life they have been waited on hand and foot, then at the point when they become the most important person in their world; you ask them to 'step up' and you wonder why they get upset with it. Step back look at the environment you have created, controlled and look at what you have taught them to be and then maybe you can see that you are trying to create a 'new normal' at a challenging time, so perhaps it needs to be a slow process that requires 'team' work. They need your support to get places and to buy things and in return you need their help to allow the family/household to work for everyone! Take time and navigate a way through that supports you all.

- **Family time**

How do you create this?

Are you able to recognise your teen's needs in wanting more independence without taking it personally?

Can you support your teen so that family time becomes a treat not a chore, it might be watching a film, a daily meal together, quality time every few days together, make it simple and fun, not pressurised. **Definitely** without elements of guilt thrown in.

- **Sport / clubs / instruments & commitments**

We teach our teens all they know, so how we are is how they may become unless we enable them to grow through our weaknesses. Many kids play sport to differing degrees and over the years I have heard teens say the hardest part is when their parents criticise them and instead of checking in with the teen they tell them what they should have done, making the teen feel 'less than'. They learn team spirit on the pitch but that they are 'not enough' off the pitch. How about we question them to learn for themselves, from themselves:

Name 3 things you did well today?

Name 2 things you could do differently?

Name 1 thing you wouldn't want to do again?

There starts the process of self-awareness and self -regulating.

The practice of instruments or hobbies, something we have encouraged as a parent to support the teen, can often become a place of 'battle'. How would it be to let the teen learn, 'if I don't do what I need to then I don't get the results'? As opposed to a 'war zone' which stops the hobby being pleasurable and instead becomes a torture for everyone involved.

Take moments to 'pause' and look outside of all that is happening in the moment and create the environment where everyone learns and grows.

• Language, tone and ways of communicating

Notice the way you speak to yourself, your partner, your teen, your friend and your colleagues, becoming aware that the people that may mean less to you get the best, polite and patient you. How you talk to your teen becomes their internal voice, so you get to be the conscious coaching voice, or you get to be the critical parent, and that is the voice they speak to themselves in until they choose to change it! Would you be ok if someone spoke to you the way you do your teen? I know it is easy to lose our temper, to raise our voice, how are you with that? How are you with someone shouting at you? How will your teen feel when that that is the voice you 'save' for them?

Also watch your tone and language as you are teaching them in this way as well.

Many parents say that their teen, can be so rude to them. Really? I wonder where they have learnt that habit ? If you come back to yourself and notice where the habit starts, you can then learn with them to be respectful, open and approachable. This is the first line of communication, how you speak to them allows them to want to talk to you.

• Expressing yourself, dress sense, piercings and body adornment

As the journey continues our teen learns to express themselves and how they choose to do this can be led by others; fashion, role models, sporting stars, musicians. It takes all sorts and you may find that your teen has ways to express themselves that go against everything you have ever known. It is a good thing then to have an awareness as to what your boundaries are and how flexible you are with these or how much you are prepared to battle for the boundary! It is important to find a way to communicate where there is room for movement. Lots of parents, say 'because I said so' that only creates the teen wanting to rebel. When we work with them, pull up alongside, and talk through we teach them resolution.

- **Smoking / drinking and drugs**

Escapism – all of these habits are ones that can become addictions, ones that we use to stop 'feeling'. It is important that you have clear boundaries as to what is ok for you within your family, that therefore acts as a guide for your teen regrading what and what not to do. It is also vital to explain to teens the pros and cons of the different drugs, drink and the combinations as well as the implications on their mental and emotional health and the physical impact. The teenage brain is still in development and the impact of numerous drugs is long lasting and far reaching, a factor that I will talk about in more depth in the 'brain chapter'. Suffice to say if we create healthy and respectful boundaries then we can lead our teens towards respecting themselves and their minds and bodies.

Take time to watch 'Nathan Wall Neuroscientist' on alcohol and teens on YouTube.

- **Sex and relationships**

The teen years are the years when hormones are rampaging

through the body. Their body is changing and the chemical reactions they are sensing within can also be heightened by all that is happening around them. How can we best make this massive journey easier and more enjoyable for them? How can we as parents allow them to know themselves and respect how they are who they are?

If they understand their bodies and they respect how they are who they are, then they have a better chance of creating healthier sexual relationships. What are your earliest memories of this stage in life? What were you taught about the sexual/physical you? What do you wish you had known to support this journey? How can you create these conversations without them being cringe worthily awkward? What do you want your teen to be able to get from 'loving/learning relationships? What do you role model at this time about love & relationships?

Boundaries play a vital role in relationships, firstly the relationship with yourself, what we allow others to do with and for us, and secondly in how we relate and act with others.

This in sexual relationships is vital in creating an adult who knows they have a right to say YES and most importantly a right to say NO!

- **Social media and interactions**

What feels appropriate to share?

Would you let your teen do what they are doing online in the physical world?

How does it impact them? Their future? What does it say about them?

Boundaries and knowing where we as a parent stand then allows the teenager a stronger understanding of the necessity of boundaries, and the role they play in keeping themselves safe in all manners. Social media is a fantastic tool if used to support life, but when it takes over and has too much power, then it can be damaging to the 'teen', an addiction to see how many likes their post has which has a significant influence their self-esteem. It can feed the teens insecurity because they can see what everyone else is doing, or portraying, even though it may not be the reality. It is so vital to take a stance, to have an opinion, even to be like the 'border patrol' and to support your teen in understanding the importance of these tools in supporting and enhancing life rather than becoming life!

- **Money, spending and earning**

Our values become their values. Our attitudes become their attitudes. We teach our teens all that they are. We have created the life they are living, so any relationship they have with money will stem from what they have seen us do, say and our interactions.

What are your beliefs about money? Where do they stem from? How would you like to change financially? What would you have wanted to know to be healthier financially?

Financially the world presents so many different messages to our teens. The world shows them that money buys you happiness and the perfect body which in turn gets you the perfect relationship and lifestyle. Social media, marketing and fashion encourages that the right trainers, phone, laptop etc will take away all your worries and bring you the life that is fulfilling. Is this the right message? What is the message you want your teens to know?

- **Friendships**

Life is enhanced by the quality of our friendships! A friend is a person that sees us and allows us to be who we are. To be a teen and to grow through the struggles of friendships can be so difficult. You are unsure of who you really are and then you have people you care about behaving in sometimes very hurtful ways. To top it all off in today's world you have the added weight of social media and the judgement, perfection, gloating and competition that comes with it.

- **Emotions, distress and support**

Our emotions play a massive role in our wellbeing, and how we are able to feel, then allows us to be able to manage them. If our emotions are ignored and suppressed, they can become mental health issues. A part of being a parent is to understand how we deal with our emotions and what we allow, teach and model to our children, for our teens to feel.

By allowing and supporting our teens to grow through the challenges of life they learn to build resilience and therefore it is imperative they learn, otherwise we have flaky adults who do not have the skills to navigate their way through the world effectively.

We all feel the world so differently and we all have a differing perspective on experiences. Your teen will feel their world differently!

What emotions are you comfortable, uncomfortable, accepting, allowing of?

How do you share how you feel?

What would you like to do differently emotionally?

Do you ask for support?

Did you get good enough emotional support as a teen?

Are you able to hold a 'space' to let your teen feel their feelings?

Do you listen well?

Do you try and problem solve?

Are you able to just be with how they are, or do you have to fix it?

Do you know when to say yes and how to say no?

Can you set wise and loving limits that your teen is able to understand and clearly relate to the reasoning behind?

Understandably many parents find it too uncomfortable to see their teens sad, disappointed, hurt or struggling in any way. This discomfort can make it difficult for both the parent and the teen to be able to access all that they need in order to get the necessary support. They lose their capacity to help by feeling overwhelmed or disconnected from their feelings. Anger can be a common reaction to situations, as the parents reaches for the most easily accessible emotion. Emotions play a most powerful role in our lives. They are the weather in our physical world. As a parent it is vital that we are aware of our emotional strengths, weakness' and blind spots.

We don't always know what our boundaries, beliefs and values are until we are made to face them, and when this is presented to us by an upset, confrontational or emotional teen, it can be challenging in many ways. If we take the time to understand what we stand for we can then communicate from a place of calm knowledge as opposed to an emotional, reactionary place that creates an unnecessary 'battle/war.'

Boundaries are guidelines for you to know what is acceptable and what is not in your life!

Emma Disney

Space for notes:

Co-dependent, Independence through to interdependence

When we become parents, especially for the first time, we have to learn the needs of a new-born and understand what it is they require to allow them to feel content and happy. We have to learn to decipher cries and movements. We have to learn routines. To understand what we want to do as a parent other than the basics of survival, we have to learn how to do this whilst going through the most major, natural but life changing event ever, one of the biggest changes in our lifetime. There is no easy way to become a parent but to become one, and a lot of what we do is what we have been taught through how we were parented. The quality of our parenting can depend on how we were parented! It is the most important role within our life, we are creating the next generation, the future, and yet how many of us actually look at how the future is shaping up and give our kids skills to enhance the world and society, to support them and enhance how well they can grow to be. We can get lost in the frenetic pace of our life, of social media, of the messages of the marketers, our careers and we can lose the joy of the **journey of becoming** for our teen, through our journey of unbecoming!

The most important ingredient to co-creating an interdependent teen is that they feel and know they are unconditionally loved and safe at home, that they are free to be authentic in how they are who they are, that the love encourages the will to be self- driven and to thrive.

As a parent it is up to us to really empower our kids by appreciating that they need to fail, get lost, not get in the team etc. They will benefit from being let down, sad, and disappointed by the world around them. If they know that someone always has their back, then they can find the way to rise again… They have to learn through failing, as failing is an important part of life; to fail, to learn to rise again!

'Fall down seven times, stand up eight times.', Japanese proverb

Teach our teens to learn by doing, by feeling, by being! There is no easy short cut. No amount of technology will allow them to develop interdependence. No amount of academic qualifications makes them resilient. Through engaging in life, in failure, in attempting, in stepping out of their comfort zone, in making connections both good and bad, in learning to trust their judgements, in understanding that their biggest enemy may well be their own mind and over thinking can they grow. By helping them to recognise, to be aware, to feel gratitude in each day we allow them to become responsible for their actions and their consequences.

Co-dependency is an emotional and behavioural condition that affects an individual's ability to have a healthy mutually satisfying relationship. Some of the signs of being co-dependent are:

- Have an excessive and unhealthy tendency to rescue and take responsibility for other people.
- Derive a sense of purpose and boost your self-esteem through extreme self- sacrifice to satisfy the needs of others
- Choose to enter and stay in lengthy and high cost care taking and rescuing relationships, despite the cost to you or others
- Have a pattern of engaging in well-intentioned but ultimately unproductive unhealthy helping behaviours such as enabling

Co-dependency usually starts in childhood. A child might have had to learn to suppress their needs due to the needs of the unstable parent, having to take on adult responsibilities, known as parentification. If your care givers/parents needed to control you, or convinced you abuse or neglect was love, then you will have learnt co-dependency. It is therefore our role as a parent and how we love that initially shapes how healthily our teens learn to love. **We as their parents are the child's first loving relationship.**

Many co-dependent people do not recognise how unhealthy their relationships are, to them they are normal. It is too easy especially for the main care giver to become co-dependent with their child, to need to rescue, make it alright, limit the reality of life, but all that is happening is limiting the growth of the teen. Many parents don't want to share 'feelings' or talk openly and honestly about certain situations, whether it is loss, death, or divorce. The teen learns not to share to ensure they make it alright for the parent, so what you have is a shutdown relationship where the people involved believe they are making it alright, rescuing the other from 'pain'.

Take time to reflect on how you were parented, to acknowledge how you learnt to love and be loved;

- What is healthy love to you?
- Do you feel loved? Loveable?
- Are you able to receive and give?
- What has caused you to be uncomfortable with receiving?
- Do you know how to give? What would you need to learn to give?
- Do you ensure everyone needs are met above yours?
- Do you enable your kids to be independent?
- What was your mothers' love like? How did it make you feel?
- How was your father with loving you?
- How was your parents love to witness?
- How would you want to have been loved differently?
- If you could describe your loving relationships what words would you use?

- Do you know what needs you meet what you don't?
- Do your kids know how to love you?
- What love do your kids witness? How would they describe it?
- Can you recognise elements of how you love as unhealthy?
- How can you change these elements that no longer serve you?
- What would you want your teen to know about healthier love?

When we take time to reflect, it is easy to recognise that love is like learning to walk. We have picked it up without acknowledging of how we actually learnt to do it, and then it becomes an unconscious process until we hit a problem, something falls apart or we watch our teen enter relationships and we see our loving acted out! As the teacher, the parent of this love, it is therefore also our responsibility to stop and to work on our love patterns, self-love programming and how we chose to interact, relate, connect and love as the first 'love relationship' our teen has is with us. We have to ensure it is healthier, more than it is not!

Independence is a massive part of the teen years, with many teens feeling the need to break free from being more closely intertwined with the family and wanting to be with their peers or on their own. Many parents take this personally as a form of rejection. What if we saw it for what it actually is? A teen wanting to understand themselves, to want to connect through discovering who they are, and that is more difficult if you have no space to be with your own thoughts, to sit in your own company, to do your own thing. How do you learn to understand yourself without space?

Independence is being able to go separate ways together, so being able to create these relationships within the family are important in guiding our teens to understand their needs as an individual. To be your own person, to be able to know your own mind and needs, to take care of yourself, to understand what you want from yourself and life is to be at ease within yourself, which in turn allows you to be driven, ambitious, motivated and to be able to connect to what you want out of this world and your life. To role model the values, beliefs and lifestyle of independence to our teens is to give them a healthy starting place for relationships. If you are happy or at ease in yourself, then any and every relationship has the opportunity to enhance you, if you allow it.

A healthy relationship is one where two independent people just make a deal that they will help the other person be the best version of themselves.

When we step back and allow our teen the space and the trust to be independent, we are allowing them to understand that this is their life and their choices, but we have their back whilst they learn to step up to become who they want to be. Interdependence is perhaps then that relating space that fits with the 'teens' need for space and independence whilst we, the parents still have their back but allow them the responsibility to be more self-reliant, more self-motivated and more self-aware!

Connection is the basis for all relationships. We want to ensure that our teen is able to have healthy relationships as these are the key stone to living a happy and fulfilled life...

Interdependence forms the base for a relationship that gives us the space to be ourselves, supports our growth, and allows us respect and flexibility with one another. Interdependence within relationships has these characteristics:

- Healthy boundaries
- Active listening
- Time for personal interests
- Clear communication
- Taking responsibility for behaviour- accountability

- Creating time and space for emotional needs
- Healthy self esteem
- Being able to be open.

All of the above are what any and every relationship that is based on intimacy requires for it to be healthy. Intimacy is to be close, familiar and affectionate. It demonstrates the togetherness and love that a family can share!

If the quality of our life is enhanced by our relationships and how we connect then as the primary care giver it is our responsibility to ensure that we are creating, role modelling and reflecting on the relationships that we both share and allow our teen to witness. If connections are the weather to our life, we need to create sunshine but learn from the storms and know that the seasons will impact us. It is our role firstly, to and with ourselves, then to and through our teen to be able to create high quality connections, then with those we invite into our lives. Where our choices are limited, family, work colleagues etc. it is up to us to teach boundaries and how they support our relationships and create healthier interactions that are constructive as opposed to destructive or toxic! We always a have a choice as to how we interact.

One of the most basic human needs is to be loved, to have love and to connect – these all start within your family environment, how you were loved, how you love, how you give, how you receive and you are each and everyday teaching through all that you do and are, through every interaction that you have what love means to and feels for you.

It is therefore of the most utmost importance that you take the time to review:

- how you got to today
- how you loved to today
- how you have been loved

- how you give love
- to work out if you had a limited amount of time on earth would you be loving differently?

As we travel the journey of life, we will experience many different types of people, relationships, interactions, connections and we can allow all of them to shape us into becoming the most connected, happy and trusting loving selves.

Many of the teenagers I have worked with crave the independence to explore themselves and their lives, but the parents find ways through their fears and insecurities to make it a really challenging time. Our teens crave independence, not control, they want us to allow them to grow, for us to believe in them and let them find their way, as a parent it is our job to look at our fears and work through them not hand them down to our kids. Many parents are programmed to think of the worst case and through this fear disempower their teen by not supporting them as they try to break free, to become more individual. It is such a vital stage in the teen years for them to learn to believe in themselves, in their decisions, and in their ability to learn from their mistakes. If they are never allowed the freedom to make their mistakes, they become trapped in a limited world and do not learn the skills they need for both survival and then to be able to thrive, so the next stage of that is older teens unable to manage life at university or as an employee as they have been taught to not trust themselves.

It is our job to set up safe boundaries, to trust our teen to do more, see more and be more. The only way that they do that is by being more self- reliant and independent; becoming more. As a parent we have to look at what it is within us that:

- Shows us this journey, what is it that we are scared off?
- What is our worrying actually doing?
- Why do we not trust our teens?

- Where do our fears stem from?
- What can you do to find calm and trust?
- What do you need to learn to let go?
- How were you trusted as a teen?
- What do you want for your teen?
- How can you create better connection whilst allowing freedom?
- Do you trust your relationship you share?
- What were your teen years like and how were you with independence?

This incredible journey of becoming, from childhood through to adulthood, grows through so many different stages. As a baby they are completely dependent upon us, needing our help to survive as they are reliant on upon us for all of their needs.

Independence is part of the teenage years, they have this need to break away from us, although on many levels it is an interdependent relationship, the teen has the biological need to feel more freedom!

Growing through and becoming the adult, our relationship becomes one of interdependence. A healthy balance of connection, freedom, trust, balance, love and empowerment. It is a balance between holding on and learning to let go in a relationship that is healthy, loving and holds and nurtures everyone involved. To witness your adult child creating a healthy relationship means that you have taught them what it is to be loved without conditions, to feel safe in the knowledge that someone has your back and you are supported with love!

Allowing our teen to grow into themselves, allows us to create a relationship based on love, acceptance and trust, that is one that is lifelong and loving!

Space for notes:

Trusting and letting go...

One of the roles of parenting is to ensure that we have taught our kids what they need to know and to do to be fully independent and to thrive in the world!

One of the most important jobs we as a parent have is to allow our kids to grow into independent young adults, to support them to believe in themselves, in allowing them to make mistakes so that they are able to become independent and confident in their choices and life.

Let us take the time to look at how we learn to be independent, how we were raised to view the world and how safe we feel in it:

- What were your parents' beliefs about your first steps of independence?
- Do you believe the world is safe or to be feared?
- Do you let your kids do age appropriate things, catch the bus, walk to town?
- What do you think is age appropriate 13? 15? 16?
- Have you taught your kids to cook? Iron? Get shopping? Do washing?
- Can your 13/14/15/16 year do ~explore what is appropriate here?
- Is your teen reliant on you to get around?
- How do you support your teens independence?
- Are you independent or do you rely on others for needs to be met?
- Are you co-dependent – is it your role to make it ok for others and that in turn makes it ok for you?
- Do you trust your teen in the world?

I meet so many kids who have the freedom to roam the virtual world in the most inappropriate ways as their parents have no real understanding of the impact of the game or the actions and consequences of the graphics or connections made through this platform. These same parents were fearful of their child walking into the local town.

The nature of how we live has changed so considerably as a result of technology. A lot of parents, not being 'digital natives', are a little unaware as to the short, medium, and long-term threats of the 'connected / disconnected' world. Our teens are able to not leave their room all day but still communicate with the outside world, they are able to view a world from their bed but make no real connection, no physical interaction.

Have we as parents let our kids down by allowing technology to be a babysitter, by using screen time to parent our children?

Have we become so distracted that we are unaware of the influence of technology on the independence of our teenager!

There is no App for life!

As much as independence is a physical reality it starts with the belief that we have in ourselves to be able to do 'something', so is it time to restart the process of looking at mental independence, emotional independence, and the power of interdependence.

Are we creating a generation who are dependent on a screen and as a result less aware of the power of independence and relationships and therefore entitled!

Kids who have been over-parented and led to believe that they can be anything they want and it will be easy have been promised the world through a fast moving and disposable lifestyle only to realise the real world requires more; to dig deeper, to try harder, to be more committed, to learn to fail and to rise, to be connected to one another through interaction. Has technology and parenting in this era diluted some very necessary skills for both the parent and the teen?

Is it time to review the integration of trust, connection and letting go and learning the necessary skills for these to happen!

Space for notes:

Competition, comparison, connection (Sport and support)

Comparison steals happiness, confidence and self-worth!

As digital-natives, our teens are made constantly aware of what every celebrity they look up to is wearing, eating, doing and subjected to what a supposedly 'successful' life looks like every second of every day. The amalgamation of social media and social competition within society is unhealthy, unrealistic and distorted in how it portrays what success is and means, what a health body looks like and what a healthy lifestyle is. We are raising kids to want to aspire to be celebrities. To be people who have done nothing but get on TV, who have achieved through the shape of their body or surgery, fillers and enhancements, who are obsessed with their looks but not their values or making a difference to our planet.

If a future generation were to look upon this time what would they be learning about us as a society? Especially where our teens are concerned!

From the very minute our teen tunes into social media they are being taught to 'want' the unobtainable. They are being shown that to be happy they have to meet certain criteria; to be this thin, to have this body shape, to be this toned, to own this, to do this... They are being bombarded with what 'will make them happy' but according to whom?

We are seeing social media stars compete for likes, aiming to get the majority of followers to define their success, and we as parents watch!

How can we wonder why self-esteem is faltering? Why anxiety is taking over schools?

Why depression is the fastest growing illness worldwide? Why suicide is becoming more normal? Why kids are feeling desperate and despairing?

Our society is teaching a happiness that is a fantasy, leading kids to want stuff that does not create happiness, but instead creates consumers. We are losing the most important element of the basic of happiness- "connection!"

- What is our role within this scenario?
- How can we best support our teen to understand their needs?
- How can we teach connection?
- What is self-connection?
- How can we foster individuality?
- What does healthy 'technology' look like?
- How do we show, role model, connection, self-esteem, happiness?
- What would your kids pick up from you with regards to values?
- How can we enhance their lifestyle?
- When do you see the impact of social media? Is it negative/ positive on your teen?
- How does technology add/take away from your life?
- How distracted are you with your phone?
- What would help you be more present?

Sometimes it is not until we are in the middle of something that we realise we have lost our way, that we need to find a new path, a healthier lifestyle. It feels like that right now we are raising a generation of kids who feel lost, overwhelmed and confused as they are swamped with messages of what success looks like and they can often be left feeling not enough.

We are living in a world where comparison is a daily habit that is eating away at our teens self-esteem and confidence. Our job is to support them to be true to themselves, to find ideas, ideals and dreams that fit with who they are, not with who they think they should be to fit in. What is happiness?

Don't compare yourself to others, the only comparison you should draw is between you and the old you!

At some level we are teaching, whether through role modelling or not preventing it, the toxic habit of comparison! We all do it whether we are conscious of it or not. Whether we are comparing how thin, rich, healthy, young or happy we are to others, or comparing things such as holidays, we are all aware of people around us and where they may have 'more than' us. Today this is life, however it is also life to accept that each and every one of us plays an important role whether it is in a 10-bedroom house with luxury or a one bedroom flat, or bedsit. No one is any better than anyone else, we are all different, but if we believe that someone who has more is better, happier, or enjoying life more we will always think less of ourselves. It is healthy to aspire and be inspired but it is toxic to compare and end up feeling less than.

Take the time to work out:

- Where in life do you feel 'less than?"
- Who, what and when do you compare yourself and how do you feel?
- What thoughts feel like they trap you with comparison?
- Do you notice how comparison makes you feel?
- How can you change your insecurities and comparison?
- Can you learn to appreciate those that you once looked up to?

The world needs people of all different shapes and sizes with all different dreams and ambitions. If we all morph into wanting the same the world becomes a bland robotic place with no personality.

Marketing tells us both us and our teens that we need X, Y and Z in order to be happy. It is up to us as the parent to teach our teen that becoming a consumer, addicted to wanting more, does not make you happy. Instead it leaves you needing to shop to get a hit, in order to feed an insecurity because you are comparing yourself to others.

Many parents compare their 'teens' and instead of celebrating who they have created and raised, they spend time thinking that other people's children are more. Observe your comparisons and ask yourself:

- What is this doing for me and my teen?
- How does this make me/them feel?
- How could I better use my brain?

If life is a journey what does the view in this part of the journey look like and where is it leading?

Competition

Life is competitive whether it is going for a job interview or a university place, we compete to 'win' what we want, whether it is a place in the school play, team, orchestra, art club, or a job! Why is it then that many schools have decided that a competitive sports day is toxic and unhealthy? Why are we teaching kids, our teens, that healthy competition is dangerous but supporting them to think toxic competition and comparison is healthy, and by this I am referring to technology and social media!

Many teens that I work with 'self- harm' through technology, comparing themselves to all that that they see on social media, craving to be like, look like someone who, frankly, doesn't deserve their time or thought. Comparing themselves to ideals, to photoshopped images that are not even real. They are showcasing themselves in 'inappropriate' clothes and poses to get likes, to get followers, to believe that they are enough. How have we created a society whereby stranger's opinions mean more than that of someone who loves you?

Selfies, gloating, over sharing:

- How can this be healthy, mentally or emotionally?
- What does this teach our teens?
- What are we setting them up for if not anxiety, insecurity and low self-esteem?

Unhealthy connection is dangerous for the mind and emotions, it erodes the sense of self, self-confidence and self-belief, dislocating the teen from themselves. As parents, it is up to us to guide, manage and inspire our teens to use technology and social media to enhance life not to create life challenging issues.

How do we do that?

We begin by understanding our relationship with technology, specifically our phones and social media. We look at what we use it for; is it to enhance or escape our lives, minds and thoughts? We become more aware of how we could change our habits and then we start to put in place guidelines as to what is expected, the 'do's and do nots. We lead our teens to understand the value, place and role of technology in their world to enhance it!

The teenage brain as I have stated numerous times is in development. It is up to us to understand what we use it for as we are creating neural pathways, habits, and addictions

We can change our brain at any time due to its 'neuroplasticity', however it is more difficult to change our habits, so why not create a relationship with technology that supports and enhances life in all ways.

Competition can be as healthy as it is unhealthy, just like eating well can support you or can become controlling and develop into an eating disorder. It is our role to teach 'balance and boundaries' and more importantly to role model what healthy competition looks like.

I have heard many kids say, 'when I get a good grade or result my parents then ask who else got that grade, and who got better results'. This is unhealthy competition. If the child wants to be inspired by a peer let them find that person and work for themselves to get better results. If you do it the underlying message is that your child is 'not enough'. The emotional needs of a teen are complex and ever changing, along with being on occasions difficult to detect. They are not themselves sometimes and do not always know what it is that they need to change how they are feeling, or what they are doing. A culture of open communication, non-judgement and positive feedback is essential. If you are going through a tough time, or being challenged in any way, what is it that you need to support you?

Comparison creates an emotional void which in turn leads to unhealthy thinking, which as we are all aware can be the start of unstable mental health. Our society has changed and is changing at such a fast pace. If it is to enhance how we are and who we are, it is up to us as parents to shape our child's daily world so that technology develops their culture, society, lifestyle, knowledge, and compassion instead of harming it.

Our values and parenting are crying out to be reviewed. Our teens mental health is in crisis with more teens being diagnosed with depression, anxiety and other mental illnesses. It would appear that the way we are living is not allowing our teen to thrive in a way they need to.

How are we going to evolve our parenting in line with the speed that the world is adapting and changing?

Space for notes:

New beginnings

**New beginnings have endings before them. Take time
to notice both components and how they allow; growth,
change and opportunity.**

When I asked the teens I know, work and live with the
most challenging parts of being a teenager a number said new
beginnings, whether that be after loss or divorce or before starting
secondary school, sixth form or university. If you think about it,
at the most unstable time mentally and emotionally in their lives,
when their brain is not fully formed, when the hormones and
chemicals are rushing through every cell in their body, the teen
has more changes to go through than at any other point in their
lives, most of which are necessary stepping stones. The teen is told
by parents, school and society that these changes are life changing
and the rest of their life depends upon the quality of their choices,
work ethic and results. Imagine the pressure of that!

- How do you feel about changes, new beginnings?
- How do you manage changes & new beginnings?
- Do you know how your teen feels about change/
  beginnings?
- What would make it easier?
- When change is on the horizon – what will support the
  process?
- What are your concerns?
- How can you manage it better?
- Does worst case thinking really help? What would best
  case thinking allow for?

Every situation that we go through we have the option to grow
through too, but very few of us will have been taught or shown
that this is choice available to us. We can allow ourselves the not
always comfortable option of growing through the challenges,

changes, losses' and separations. We can become more even when we feel less.

In order to grow we have to be brave enough to acknowledge our fears and walk, feel and grow through them.

If we can lead our teen to be 'more' themselves through any given situation we are allowing them the gift of expansion. We are teaching them not to shrink and diminish who they are when life gets tough, not to get trapped within their minds and become anxious but to flow with life and be their best selves! I believe that unless we are 'consciously' raising our teens, we are acting out of habit and we are just doing what we have always done because we have always done it that way. Is that a good enough reason?

In my role both as a mother and psychotherapist my greatest teachers have been the teens themselves. They have shared what they need, whether that was through words, tone, actions or attitudes. If I observe and feel, not react and take it personally, they give me the clues required to tell me what they need. You know your teen better than anyone else. They may have changed to a degree, but they are still the toddler or the primary school pupil they once were, they have just developed habits, skills, attitudes and behaviours which in some ways you have taught them. The teen is partly a reflection of you but acted out in their way, so if you want to see where you need to change, watch your teen. If you want to see where you are stuck in habits that don't serve you, feel where your teen triggers your emotions.

The teen years especially are about learning. There is pressure on teens academically to learn what they need to be 'successful' to get the grades to allow them to access the next step. Not all teens thrive within the school system. It is then for us to help them to see that it is ok to be different and sometimes life asks us just to do enough to get to the next stage, not everyone thrives in every situation. Schooling can have a lifelong impact if it is a negative experience, so we have a duty of care to support our teen and help them manage their academic journey to the best of their ability. Some of that may just be surviving it!

When do they get what they need to manage the lessons they are learning? Emotional and mental growth is the scaffolding to the building! What does your teen need to get through this chapter?

In order for our teens to feel at ease in themselves and within the world around them they require mental and emotional support to know the importance of feelings, change, self, resilience, responsibility, choices and their consequences. They need to understand the power of their own minds and the impact of the quality of their relationships, firstly with themselves!

Space for notes:

Chapter 5

EXERCISE AND TOOLKIT

Mindset

"**I**t is not the strongest of the species that survives, nor the most intelligent that survives. It is the one that is the most adaptable to change!", Charles Darwin

Your mindset is your collection of thoughts and beliefs that shape your thought habits. These affect how you think, what you feel and what you do. Your mindset impacts how you make sense of the world and how you make sense of you. It shapes your attitude and your attitude reinforces your mindset.

In the chapter entitled 'Rational and Emotional', I have talked about the way we think and the way it impacts our teens'. This is the next level of thinking that shapes both their and our world. 'Mindset' plays a massive role in shaping and perceiving within every day and how we respond to life. In order to support our teens and their perceptions it is helpful to check in with them, allowing them to become aware of where their thoughts are taking them too. We sometimes believe as parents that we are able to teach or tell our teens, but sometimes through questioning or challenging them gently they are able to see for themselves a different way to view the situation!

When it comes to mindsets there are two types:

- A '**fixed**' mindset is when someone believes that their basic abilities, intelligence and talents are fixed traits.
- A '**growth**' mindset is a belief that all learning and intelligence can grow with time and experience.

From all that neuroscience is uncovering, neuroplasticity demonstrates that the brain grows and changes as we learn more. The brain grows with our learning. One of the most fertile periods of growth are the teenage years so it makes great sense to encourage your teen to keep an 'open mind'. Keep their mind in neutral on a regular basis!

If we can support our teen to become more aware of what they believe in but also to be able to be adaptable, then we are teaching them that their mind is ever changing and so can their outlooks. As parents we can then review how we have reached our views, beliefs, and attitudes and take space to reflect whether they serve any beneficial purpose. Our mind-set shapes our world in so many ways and is also the basis of our habits, beliefs and attitudes. Much of what we believe and do is unconscious. We usually only change as a result of a situation, as our brain is a 'pattern matching organ' that thrives from the patterns and habit of life. Our brains like to create a comfort zone and live within it!

In order to grow and live with a 'growth' mindset we have to be able to challenge ourselves and want to live differently. This sounds so much easier than it is to do. Let's take the time now to reflect and review so we can then inspire and support our teen to become an ever-evolving person who is willing to grow on a daily basis and thereby update and upgrade themselves like they do their phones!!!

Take some time to reflect on your beliefs, attitudes and see whether they still fit with you:

- How do you think of life- is it a gift or a challenge?
- Do you believe you have to work hard to achieve?
- Do you believe life owes you?
- Do you believe in your dreams?
- Do you believe you can achieve your dreams?
- Have you been taught to believe in yourself?
- Have you been taught ask for help?
- Do you think it's important to help others?
- Do you think you are enough just as you are?
- Do you believe you are loveable?
- Do you believe you are good enough?
- Do you believe you are a good enough parent?
- Do you trust your 'teen?'
- Do you believe life is what you make it?
- Are you fiercely competitive?
- Do you compare yourself?
- Do you always want more?
- Do you know contentment?
- How do you define success?
- What does happy mean to you? How do you express it?
- What does love mean, to you? How do you share it?
- How do you feel about dying?
- What are your beliefs about relationships? Friendships? Love? Intimacy?
- What is your belief about your 'purpose?'
- What is the meaning of your life to you?
- What makes you feel secure?
- What makes you feel insecure? How does that impact you?
- What allows you to feel a sense of achievement?
- How do you feel about your body & self- care?
- How do you feel about the power of your mind?

- Do you have the need for a sense of control?
- What religious or spiritual beliefs do you have & why?
- How did you come about some of your beliefs?

There are so many questions that we could ask ourselves to become more aware of how we are who we are, so maybe just take some time over the next few week or months to become more aware of where you are fixed and where you are flexible with your thoughts and attitudes....

Along with the growth and fixed mindset as a parent there is the fear based and the loving mindset.

The fear- based/ fixed mindset says:

- I have to control my teens behaviour
- My child learns through consequences and punishments
- I am the dominant figure.

Our parenting styles, when fear based, can create a teen who is anxious, fearful, or extreme in their rebellion as they have been tightly controlled as opposed to being trusted or supported in the learning process.

Another parenting style that is fear based is permissive parenting, as the parent is scared to lose their child's love and therefore has minimal boundaries so as not to upset the teen.

A loving mind-set is the healthiest parenting style, whereby you are able to be authoritative through coaching the teen to know you are there for them and hold healthy boundaries, whilst also allowing them to learn as they experience life.

The loving/growth mindset says;

- I will role model to you how best to manage life

- I will support you as you learn and step in when you ask or need it
- I will create healthy boundaries and we can review as you grow
- I will ensure that I support myself so I can fully support you
- I will be honest about my mistakes
- We will talk about what you think you need
- I will apologise when I get it wrong
- I am willing and open to learn from and with you.
- I will be accountable for me and my actions and not use blame

When we take time to reflect, we can begin to recognise how we parent, and again, it might be that we are just different versions of how we were parented. Until we take time to stop and acknowledge how we want to be and what mind-set we want to work from we are parenting unconsciously.

Choice means that we need to consciously create our mindset. To allow yourself to transition to a growth mindset widen your perspective, give yourself more windows through which to view the situation, so you are then able to reframe it.

"Insanity is doing the same thing over and over and expecting different results.", Albert Einstein

Repeating the same thought, action or behaviour over and over will get you the same result – time to make changes if you want a different outcome!

Space for notes:

Mindfulness

The art of noticing and paying attention to the present moment.

To be aware of our mind and how we are thinking and acting within our life is so powerful as it allows us to create choice. So much of life can be a sequence of unconscious habits, thoughts and actions because that is how we are and what we do. To live unconsciously, our brain, the pattern matching organ, finds comfort in habit. Habit takes away choices as we continue to live in a certain way, just because we have always lived in that way.

What if we took the time, and it is not humanly possible to do it all the time but more of the time, to live consciously? Being more aware of ourselves, our thoughts, our behaviours, our actions and reactions, then choosing responses. Becoming more aware of how you are "being human."

Take a moment and think about your morning routine:

- Do you always do the same thing?
- Do you ever change it?
- What is the routine? Why?
- Is it effective & efficient?
- What is your first thought in the morning? Why?
- What would you like to change? Why?
- How could you update your morning to support all involved?

Sometimes our habits are so old they are like friends, but these friends don't always support us. What if we were able to regularly sit down and reflect on how mindful we are in our life and how we could use mindfulness to parent our teen;

- Be more present with ourselves, our feelings and give ourselves time

167

- Slow life down where we are able, stress less
- Take time out from technology to witness all around us
- Make time to be together
- Listen and feel all that is being said, shared and acted out
- Learn not to take things personally, sit with the feelings
- Honour the feelings and share them
- Take time alone to recharge and reconnect, quiet time
- Turn screens off to allow for space to connect
- Make meal-times sacred to share
- Phone free rooms
- Teach teens to feel, to learn to sit with not push away feelings instead noticing them
- Notice thoughts and how you respond to them and share with your teen
- Interact with your teen throughout all their 'moods' check in with them
- Learn to navigate difficult conversations and share how it feels
- Create new experiences and share them with your teen
- Ask your teen questions as to how they are thinking, feeling
- Help them to be aware of their surroundings, the sky, mother nature.
- Learn together that being present allows for a better quality of life
- Where do you think you could use mindfulness as a parent to support you?
- What is the biggest trigger for you as a parent?
- What is a flashpoint in your parenting day?
- What can you start with for you to become more aware?

Mindfulness allows us, the parent, to be more aware of how we are in the present moment. This allows us to catch ourselves as we **react**, giving us choices as to how we can **respond** to our teen. It is the basic foundation to create healthier relationships, foundations, routines and connections so that we show our teen that there is always a choice in every given situation. When we are mindful, we have created the headspace to take the time to feel, connect and then allow ourselves to be with all that is, as opposed to using old habits to unconsciously react. By using mindfulness, we create a neural pathway that allows for us to choose as oppose to react out of habit. To respond mindfully is to evolve and give our self the gift of a growth and loving mindset!

"When we are no longer able to change a situation, we are challenged to change ourselves." Man's Search for Meaning, Viktor Frankl

Space for notes:

The journey, journaling, connection and empathy

On this journey of life, we are all experiencing every step of the way as a unique individual. No matter how close we are to someone each step of our journey is entirely ours. It is for us to make this journey as rich, loving, caring, warm and full of the texture of life as we possibly can. This in turn creates a healthy lifestyle that impacts on those around us, so it can have a powerful and inspiring knock on effect. However, a bit like cooking if you have not got the right ingredients to start with, then the desire to make something and the reality are miles apart. What is the recipe for a journey that is both emotionally and mentally healthy?

Well, it starts with how you were parented and loved and what you know to be true! If your parents, like all humans, had emotional or mental wounds and had not healed then they too pass this on, as they do the language you now speak. They unconsciously share their pain with you in how they love, feel, communicate and connect. It becomes an inherited way of being until someone stops and takes time to work on themselves, just like you are doing now; taking time to invest in the healing of your family by understanding your role within the family dynamics at this time and with your teen.

There are many ways we can create and teach the connection with our teens. One of the most valuable tools that, I believe, can help anyone is to journal; to take a blank page and to write out how we feel, to sit with ourselves and to check in:

How do I feel mentally, emotionally and physically?

How is this situation/experience making me feel?

What is it bringing up for me?

What are the ways through this?

When we sit with our self, we connect with our self, we learn the wisdom that we have picked up, we listen to ourselves, we start the next level of self -trust, awareness and develop a relationship with our self.

A conversation Journal is also powerful, use a journal to share our thoughts and feelings and pass it between whoever it is we want to share with. It becomes a place of trust, a book of insights, creating a sense of intimacy that feels safe and is accessible as and when needed.

Connection is the most powerful, nurturing and necessary part of parenting, for our child needs to feel they belong, that they are seen, that they matter. It all starts with the relationship you share, so how you connect to them teaches them how to connect with others. You are role modelling the way they will connect, feel connected and create relationships, so maybe take time to notice what it is you do to allow your teen to feel seen, heard, and known. Do you make time to sit with them, do you check in with them?

Success can be defined in so many ways, as a mother and psychotherapist, my idea of success is to be able to do my work on me, creating a healthy life, so ensuring my kids don't inherit my pain because I am aware that my parenting will create its own dynamics! Success feels like raising myself to heal and raising my children consciously when I am able.

To consciously parent is not possible all of them time, and when I become unconscious in my behaviour I can react. When this happens, it is important to take time to reflect on, own up to and apologise for my behaviour allowing my kids to see that I am being aware and doing my best when able! To role model empathy and foster connection allows my kids to be seen and heard and then for me to have the open mindedness to support them to be themselves, not a version of me or what I have dreamed for them!

When life is full of so much, and the world is telling our teens that to be more they must have more, it is important to teach our teens gratitude. If we live with gratitude we teach that we are enough just as we are, that they are enough just as they are and when we are grateful for all that we are and have, then we can enjoy the journey of life in a very different and more fulfilling way.

The journey is about 'becoming' for our teen – becoming the happiest, healthiest, most authentic self who is confident, calm, loving and learning to be at ease in themselves and the world today; to be connected to their heart and to be able to be aware of others, to be empathetic!

"We need a worldwide initiative for educating heart and mind in this modern age. We need to place greater values on our inner values, teaching love, compassion, forgiveness, justice, mindfulness, tolerance and peace." Dalai Lama

What is it that they need from us?

They need us to show up and be present....

How do you want to show up/be present within your family?
To your family?
With your friends?
With your partner?

Can we show up and show them that life throws curve balls, that we do get hurt, that it does not always work out as we want, that dreams get lost, and people step out of our lives, that some friends become enemies and some enemies become friends, that some days we may have to drag ourselves though and others we can embrace with love? If we do this whilst being connected to our authentic self, being true to who we are, being brave in our honesty to feel and being courageous in loving and healing then we un-become our wounds and we role model a life of endless potential. We then we allow for limitless living and unlimited possibilities.

If we aim to create an environment that is about growth, evolving, healing and being and a journey of texture, feeling and glimpses, moments and relationships that enhance us! The journey today as a teen looks on the world as being so very competitive, based on comparison, on how many likes, on what they own, wear, have or the pressure to get grades to succeed, to aim to be something. All of this whilst a lot of the time being connected to a portal of distraction that is based on 'more' and on what everyone else is doing whilst you are not. How can this create young people that feel enough in themselves?

It is our role to find ways to teach the next generation about the 'healthiest self', the part of them that has to connect to themselves first before they connect to anyone else or a device.

Let's explore how you do that and then you will have an insight as to how to make changes as a role model to establish healthy connections:

- How do you disconnect from your devices?
- How often do you 'switch off?'
- Are there times, rooms, places where technology is banned?
- What do you do to take time for your mental health?
- How do you check in emotionally with yourself?
- What support do you have in place mentally and emotionally?
- Physically, how do you let off steam?
- What are your beliefs for your kids?
- What are your parenting beliefs?
- How and who do you connect to?
- When do you feel connected to your teens?
- What do you do to create connection time?
- How do you empty or still your mind?
- Do you take breaks from social media, or do you unfollow people?
- Are you aware of the impact of social media on your teen?

On a physical journey, we check we have enough fuel in the car, or a ticket to travel. We pack snacks, drinks and have an idea of our destination. We may add our favourite tunes to enhance the journey or chose a route that is quickest or perhaps easier. We take time to plan. Can we now transfer these skills to organizing our mind and our life?

How do you plan your life journey, mentally and emotionally?

How do you prepare for stages of it?

Do you ensure you have the appropriate support, equipment and understandings?

Do you keep an open mind with regards to optional routes?

Life is the journey and the journey is our life, there is no destination but to travel the path. If this is the case then surely it is for us to make the journey whatever we need it to be, whether that is fun, exploring, calm, healing or feeling. Allow yourself time to explore what this stage in your journey is all about and discover how best you can meet your needs so in turn you can meet those of your teen.

Many of my teen and adult clients whilst in therapy have discovered the power of journaling; to sit with yourself and to become the explorer of your feelings and your thoughts by uncovering them through writing. Initially they will tell me how they don't really write and it's not something they would do, but after the resistance and us sharing that until they started therapy, they probably did not talk about their feelings much either. I ask them to just allow themselves time, to not judge and to just empty their heart and mind onto a page. What follows is a beautiful unravelling of themselves, of their understandings, of their insights, of their journey and this allows them the reflection to see themselves in a way that becomes enriching.

As a teen a journal can become a safe space, a time and place when they sit with themselves, their feelings, their discomfort, their confusion, pain and perhaps the conflicts that are around and within and just 'witness' their truths. No external feedback is needed just the realisation that this is who they are in this moment and this is how it feels. By acknowledging it, just that alone allows for deep healing and change within.

"The curious paradox is that when I accept myself just as I am, then I can change.'
Carl Rogers – On Becoming a Person

Connection and empathy then are the richness to life, they are the emotional threads that when weaved throughout life, throughout each experience they enhance how we feel and even when it is a challenging or difficult situation, we can use both of them to support us in our growth and development.

To connect to ourselves firstly allows insight into how we feel and what is a happening for us and then we can choose to connect outside to ask for help. When we do this, we allow our teen the understanding that life can feel challenging, difficult and that is a part of life and we can use both our emotions and connection to grow through these times.

Space for notes:

Things teens want their parents to know:

Charlie B

I'm not always not feeling okay, or good, but it's okay to not always be okay (if that makes sense). Sometimes we just need time to figure things out on our own, but have you close enough by that we know that if we need you, you are there.

I want my parents to acknowledge the fact I have struggled in the past and had bad days. I would want them to be aware of certain things or situations that would not necessarily trigger but I would find extraordinarily difficult or not be able to actually do and so they would not intentionally place me in said position again.

Not sure this one applies to others as well – but sometimes a little reassurance or a little bit of affection (not too much especially for me) just to know that they're proud of you or they love you and them not be forced to say it would always go a long way, especially for me anyways.

C B

What I wanted my parents to know when I was growing up was simple, I wanted them to know me. Obviously, they love me, but I never felt like there was the proper connection that one expects from family.

I understand the drive of my parents, they sent me to private school and provided me with most things financially any person could want in order to try and give me a better start in life than they ever had. I am forever grateful however, while providing me with what I wanted, this did not provide me with what I needed. Interaction was usually limited to the weekends, but no adult really wants to spend all weekend with their children exclusively.

Sadly, now I realise that this lack of communication on an

emotional level with my parents hindered me in later life. I felt like they did not understand me, I felt that I could not talk to them beyond the usual love woes and exam difficulties. A situation came to a head in my late teenage year that I was unable mentally or emotionally to deal with. I now have the tools to deal with my issues to the point where I'm now perfectly fine if still not always able to deal with some challenges I know who to go to and how to process and deal with them.

This lack of emotional connection does still prevail to a lesser extent to this day, this can be emotionally draining especially when you feel like your emotions matter less. Now, as I said, it is lessened. To this day as I suspect my parents try at least to make more of an effort considering what I put them through. I suppose that emotional distance is ingrained and hard to fight.

I wanted to feel known, for who I was and what I was thinking, rather than having the idea that he has a tv or an Xbox so he must be fine and happy. This is what society tells you, if you want to be happy you need material possessions. No, what I wanted was emotional possession. I wanted my parents to play with me, to listen to me, to take stock in what I was saying and not place me out of conversations when older people came over. I just wanted them to take more of an interest in me and what I was doing. I felt distanced from them to an extent.

I guess the point I'm trying to make is this while we live in a materialistic world that's driven by consumerism and the ideals of money, that's worth completely fuck all when it comes to your kids. I guarantee you your child would be happier with you taking them down the park, playing ball rather than buying them a phone or something to distract them. It distances you from your kids, and them from you emotionally. That emotional connection is vital, it makes the communication of issues easier and it helps us understand each other better. This could go a long way to help with severe depression as the main reason for depression is the feeling that no one is listening.

Basically, you can have all the money in the world and work hard to provide a life and things for your children that you never had but nothing will compare to you spending time and taking an interest in them.

H D

I think one thing I would like parents to know is when we are grumpy it is not just because we are a teenager and that we are hormonal, it is just because we sometimes get grumpy as adults do too.

I also feel like parents say, "Oh my teenage son is so lazy all he ever does is watch tv". Which we clearly know is not the case. Sometimes school can be stressful and to just watch a bit of tv and relax can help.

Some parents think that teenagers are stuck to their phones. They sometimes have a point, but we can live without our phones. For example, when I am at my cousin's house, I am only on my phone is to put music on or to show them a funny video. I think we only go on our phones because we can sometimes feel awkward and uncomfortable in certain situations and it makes us feel safe because it is a distraction. I also think we go on our phones because it is a habit when we get bored.

I think parents sometimes need to understand that we are teenagers and we are learning. We learn from our mistakes and we are going to do some stupid things in this huge learning process.

D E

One thing I always hated was when adults would undermine me, like how am I supposed to grow up if you're treating me like I'm a toddler? You know what I mean? It is rather patronising and frustrating. I get some parents, like my mum, who don't really want their child to grow up but, I mean, we have to, especially in our teen years, it's rather important we learn how to grow up, so forcing us not to is rather silly.

We need freedom to make mistakes and learn from them but also not too much freedom, so we have discipline too. Parents need to be less paranoid about their children. I have many mates whose parents sheltered them their entire childhood/teen years so now they're too nervous and too quick to judge everything. On the other end of the spectrum I know kids whose parents didn't give a shit and they're a total mess.

J B

Times have changed since they were younger, things I'd share to parents are:

- Don't censor or screen us from real life
- Let us learn from our mistakes and grow through them
- Let us be left alone until we need help
- Sometimes we just need to talk and have support from our parents, not intervention
- In some situations, don't try too hard to talk or fit in with us, just let it happen naturally
- When annoyed or upset don't pin us down or bomb us with questions. Either leave us or help us
- Teach us about your past so we can learn from it
- Have a relationship with us
- If we lash out it is not always us, hormones take over
- We're going through what you had to, don't pretend you were any better than us
- We are still growing, still "kids"
- Society these days is very hard to fit it and is very complicated (social media)
- Don't be paranoid, let us do our thing

- Support us in what we do and lead us in the right direction, but not by the hand
- Don't shout and scream at us, does not help
- Most of the time we just want to be left alone
- We are grateful for what you do for us in every aspect
- Often it is hard to show emotions to our parents
- If we don't talk to you or seem pissed off does not mean we're annoyed at you or or having a bad time, it's just hormones and how we are growing up

Sadie M

In my opinion I would like it if parents would listen to me rather than hear the first point I have to say and kick up a fuss without hearing my other ideas and points. I would like them to listen to everything I have to say and then explain, without being patronizing, their ideas because if they try and start an argument right away it's just going to cause aggravation on both sides and will most likely end up in a huge row which could have been easily avoided.

I also don't agree with parents throwing things back in your face. For example, in my year many kids get expensive gifts or just basic items for nothing, such as clothes or shoes, and I know this because it is posted on social media. Most of my friends argue with their parents about silly things like clothes and shoes, but it is a big thing as others are judged for what they wear. If I was to ask for a pair of shoes or clothes my mum would be quick to point out that she bought me clothes at the start of the summer, but it is coming close to winter. It's very annoying when parents don't understand why you need new clothes or shoes.

I think that parents need to understand that school sometimes isn't the nicest place to be, as I have seen some people being bullied and what is said or done to them is horrendous.

I also think parents should not compare their children as they are both different people with different personalities. My mum does occasionally compare me to my brother, which I think is quite frustrating as me and my brother will never end up with the same life so to compare me to him, I think is actually an insult because we are not alike in any way and even though he has got good qualities he has also got bad ones, like me, which I wouldn't want attached with my name or for people to know me by.

I think tons of arguments could be avoided if parents understood the child's perspective.

Angel

As a child something that seems so small can have such a big impact! I felt so hurt, it broke my heart every time I didn't feel seen, it hurt me. I just wanted time, attention, love and kindness and that was too hard! I felt sad and disappointed, I chose to believe again, and I felt I was let down again, I now know that this was not personal to me.

I wish parents would make up their mind about age, one minute I am old enough to know better, and the next minute that I am not old enough. Parents attitude can destabilise a child, they are the anchor the only constant in life, so they play a massive role in stability. I know that I am 18 but I still want to be parented, I still want to feel that you have my back, that you are my safe place. Sometimes I think you forget that I need you. I crave your love, support and time with you. I need you more that I think you are aware of. I recognise that as the eldest I have played the role of a parent and in doing so have the lost the luxury of being parented. On some level I recognise that emotionally my needs changed a long time ago, life changes new relationships and families are created, I have had to learn to adapt to fit in. The family changes have felt chaotic at times, destabilising and I got dragged into every new relationship, met new partners and all the time felt unseen in so many ways. I am gutted that I had to grow up too fast.

Questions that parents want answers to:

I would like to know how to handle my emotions when they get angry, yell, roll their eyes, say hurtful things and are basically impossible to live with. I would love some tools to be able to remain in control of my emotions when faced with their yoyo ones?

I have found from both working with teens and my own teens that when they lose it, when the most emotional part of their brain kicks in they are in 'reaction' mode, acting unconsciously, and whilst still accountable for their words and actions it must be understood that when in a stable emotion none of these words and actions would cross their mind. It is all too common for us at this point to reflect that back and to lose control… So it is at this time that we have to PAUSE… to practise the PAUSE, to take a step back, to walk away and count to 10, 100, 1000 whatever it is we need to in order to calm down to regain our balance and to find the place to conjure a RESPONSE. All too often our reactions are habits and sometimes they are learned behaviour from how we were parented, so it is up to us to relearn new habits to create healthier relationships with our teen and calmer lives for ourselves. Like any new skill, it takes practise, if you are to learn a new language you now you have to practise this is exactly the same…. You are creating new neural pathways. You will also be teaching your teen to be calm in the midst of stress as opposed to reaction.

"SOMETIMES NO RESPONSE IS A RESPONSE AND A POWERFUL ONE!"

I would like to know what would be the implications if I were to just 'put up with it' and let them run their lives, would my life be calmer because I would have 'let go' versus 'get involved'?

There is a difference between responding, reacting and putting up with. If you were to put up with certain behaviours, or attitudes, then you are teaching your kids that it is ok to behave that way. Perhaps it is knowing what feels right to let go of and what feels too important not to address. As a therapist it is knowing which boundaries are too important to ignore and which skills the teens will need to have to survive and thrive in the outside world.

"PICK YOUR BATTLES, YOU DON'T HAVE TO SHOW UP TO EVERY SITUATION YOU ARE INVITED TO."

I would like to understand a bit more why they refuse any discussions about their behaviour, as 'they are perfect, and it is the parent that knows nothing'... So there is not dialogue?

Kids often behave like one or both of their parents or caregivers, so if one of you is unable to hear criticism, is always right or stubborn, or won't listen to feedback then they might behave the same way. Also, it is how we address the issue. Would you hear what you are trying to say to your teen? I know that many teens are highly insecure about who they are so then to be told that they are 'not enough' can put them in a position of defend/attack. Maybe asking them, if I have an issue and we need to talk how best is it to share with you?

All that we are sharing with our kids is all that they will then use in the outside world. Are we making them feel safe and that we are their cheerleaders, or do they feel that no matter what they do the they are under attack? As a mum, sometimes when I am grumpy, I can easily throw my mood at them, so we have to be aware of what is ours and when it is appropriate to share our thoughts with them!

I would like to understand why they go from giving kisses in primary (June) to 'drop me off at the corner' in middle school (2 months later). Why so embarrassed about their parents when they change from little to secondary school? Why is not 'cool' to be around your parents?

The teen years are about their peers, about fitting in about being more independent, about breaking away from being a child and becoming more of who they are. It is a necessary part of the 'growing up' process to separate, to be more them. As a parent, it is for us to accept this necessary emotional development and not take it personally. It is not that we are not enough, it is that they need more or less.

Why do they go from nice, very polite young people to very rude, talking back, and rolling their eyes even when we just open our mouths?

Some of the changes are due to the structure of their brain and just how much change is going on within it. If you imagine a snow globe and that someone is shaking it really, really, hard but you are trying to see what is inside, you will know it is all 'uncertain' – well this is the teenage brain, add on top of that huge influxes of hormones and you have the 'brainstorm' of being a teen all of that within a body that is changing shape, voices that are all over the place, the pressure of school and friends and parents that want you to step up. It is the most chaotic time in life so far, internally and what they need is extra support, understanding and love and what we as parents do is see a growing young adult and ask even more of them…. Hence the attitude!

I would like to know how to keep calm and remain rational. For me, a big challenge is letting them do things their way (as it is usually different to mine and I am a bit of a controlling type person). I would like to know what boundaries (which seem to, dynamically and daily, need to be adjusted) are fair to keep them in line yet give them their freedom.

The issue is to control, and that is what will cause so much stress and conflict. How do they become themselves if we are always telling them to be like us because we know more? We don't know more, we know more of our way. So how about finding a middle ground? Maybe you can learn a different way by keeping an open mind. I have written in an earlier chapter all about boundaries. We need to have differing levels of boundaries for different areas in life, so if manners and tidiness are vital to happiness for you then your boundaries might be concrete in these areas, and if you are ok with these being areas of conflict, then it is a choice.

For me as a therapist, it is working with each teen and finding out what matters, what is important, what is the cost and consequence, and finding a compromise. Teaching the teen to meet in the middle is a great skill for both parent and child.

For me as a parent, learning that my way is not always the right way for my teen and being open to learn a new way is vital, and with regards to boundaries and balance it can be a daily process as each day we are all in different head-spaces but it is knowing that we can find a way through, that can be calmer.

I would like to know, does this phase end? Why is it here now and how can I be confident it is going to end and that one day we will have a more calm, respectful relationships?

This phase does change when people find new ways through the situations, it won't end until new behaviours are found, all it will do it continue to develop rifts and the control will become toxic to all involved – what would you do if this was happening in a friendship?

Make a plan between you and your teen as to what the boundaries are – meet half-way!

It sounds to me that you are a strong woman, who has taught your kids to be just as strong and on a daily basis you are all playing different levels of 'tug of war' – where often no one wins everyone just feel emotionally and mentally exhausted.

I have a silly mantra that I try to repeat but maybe there is something better? My mantra is 'the cake is not finished baking yet ...' (I've pulled the cake out and the knife is not clean meaning, they are not children but people in the middle of being made so not to worry, the cake will one day be baked).

I love the mantra and all I would add to it is – have you used the right ingredients, as if it is plain flour it won't rise- so maybe the mantra can now be.

"Have I used the right ingredients, the right quantities, and now to trust that at the right temperature and for the right time, my cake will be baked and ready to enjoy!"

How to stay sane?

Self-care is vital. So many parents neglect themselves and give everything to their families, jobs, homes and friends and then wonder why they feel like they are going mad. Self-care looks different for everyone, but I believe I have covered it in a few of the chapters.

"Be your own best friend, if that's a challenge, be a good friend to yourself."

I would like to know strategies to be able to help

my teenager. As a parent you become overwhelmed, emotionally and physically drained, very alone and isolated thinking it's only happening to you. You've done something wrong. Watching your child go from happy, care-free to anxious, angry, overwhelmed. Not having access to the right help, knowledge, strategies to help your teenager and the rest of the family.

I hope that this book has answered this statement, as I know so many parents go through, blaming themselves that they must have done something wrong to have a teen that is experiencing issues and behaving out of character. We can only do what we know, and we are given so little information as to how to parent best especially in this digital age. We are all learning as we go along. So, perhaps step back and stop judging yourself so harshly and share with others your journey. I do think there is a need for space for parents to decompress in an environment where they feel seen, heard and not judged.

I would like to understand the enormous changes teenagers go through mentally - the changes to their brain. Not the scientific stuff. Clear, simple explanations.

Again, I hope I have fully explained just how extraordinarily difficult the adolescent stage is with regards to the brain and its incredible development at this time. There are also other books, Youtube channels and many specialists who share their knowledge on social media, explore.

Anger - the hardest part to deal with was the anger – emotional and physical. And not knowing how a child could go from calm, seemingly happy to full blown anger.

Because the teen brain is acting from the most sensitive and emotional part, there is no logic to the reactions, it is pure emotion, so the teen does not have the structural equipment to be rational. The only way to develop a calmer teen is to be the calm, the anchor, so as and when they explode it is to be calm at that time and then afterwards talk to them about how they can do this differently and in a way that works better for them to get their needs met. It is almost that we emotionally coach them to see they do have choices and to PAUSE and find that place of behaviour to respond from.

Support in the home to help deal with the issues. Support from others who understood and got it. Support in understanding what you as a family were going through - that's on all levels as a parent (the feeling of failure) to supporting siblings.

An area that is vital, we start to look into developing to create a healthier environment for families to grow through and heal after trauma and challenges of some teenage behaviours.

Support for the teenager that was not constrained to normal counselling sessions. A safe place for them to explore, talk, BE, understand and work through what was happening. A safe place for them to hang out and live life.

Maybe a future project!

Above all is the lack of knowledge, lack of support, compassion.

I hear you and really believe that as parents maybe it is time we started to change how we share our journey to allow for all of the above to be incorporated firstly in our lives so we feel supported, and secondly to create environments where teens can explore their challenges in a way that feels kind, developing and safe.

Advice on how to keep communication channels more open?

Know what it is that you need when you feel emotional and vulnerable and become this for your teen. Keep an open mind where possible and instead of thinking you have the answers, which is so easy as a parent, allow yourself to explore their thoughts and opinions and ask them what it is they need from you, to listen, advice or more!

How best to approach touchy subjects such as: inappropriate dress sense, bad language, friends we disapprove of, drugs, smoking, drinking?

As a therapist, the one thing that I have witnessed, is when parents have a strong opinion about what they disapprove of it is like giving the teen the green flag to do those things, so maybe take the route of education. Educate your teen as to the consequences and how these things might play out in their life, and show them, share with them the stories of worst case, so they can see why you have the opinions you do. As a mum I explained to my teen son, drugs and their impact, why people take them, firstly to appear cool, to get out of their heads, literally and then I explained addiction along with worst cases for each and every drug and what they do to the brain. I then gave him permission to take whatever he wanted to, all of a sudden there is no act of rebellion instead there is the reality of worst case, not such an adventure if worst case is serious mental health issue! I am not saying this is always the way to go but it has worked for me and with clients and parents. Explain the different pathways if life is clean and healthy, balanced or has addiction and drug usage!

How to make myself the therapist and confidante as well as the parent?

Be open, listen non-judgementally, hear what they are saying and do your best not to give advice or your experience let them show you who they are!

Learn about how they view their world without assuming you know!

Be curious!

What do you find to be the most challenging areas? My teen closes up when I talk about anything sensitive and

then tries to walk out of the room- how do we make time and space to talk?

I have found when working with teens that talking to their parents can feel too much, especially if the talking can end in disagreements or can become overwhelming in differing ways. There are many ways to start conversations that can feel less intense, perhaps through text, email or in a place where it is not looking at one another, so driving in the car or whilst in the kitchen doing something else. It is important to remember that the teen brain is working from the most emotional part so any kind of vulnerable or reactive chat is emotional to your teen. Your job to make it easier, calmer and safe for your teen to share.

Making a comment about something I disapprove of without it sounding like I am 'judging' - I would like to know how to make it sound like good advice?

This situation sounds like a hand grenade waiting for the pin to be pulled. Perhaps you have the option to say, "I hear you and it sounds like you have an idea that is out of my comfort zone", so you make it about you being uncomfortable as opposed to you disapproving!

Choice of clothes - I have been too soft and now have a daughter who dresses inappropriately with no clue seemingly about what looks good/right for certain occasions and weather?

Another situation where it is a learning curve for all involved, you have choices here, to do the same as you always do and it feels like it ends up in conflict, or you can let her experiment and it is then she learns what is appropriate through trial and error! Maybe making it 'your alright' is not alright for her!

My daughter has said she wants her nose pierced, multiple piercings in her ears, 5 tattoos…where will it stop? I find my blood boiling when I hear her aspirations. I find it so hard to say calmly that it's unattractive & permanent and she might regret it later in life, then I struggle with the fact that maybe it should be her choice not mine and she should love and learn.

I hear that your daughter is adventurous and wants to experiment, but from what you have shared she is still too young to have these done so what about if you explore why it gets you so emotional and upset and heal the rage and then just acknowledge what it is she wants to do in 3-4 years and who knows she may have changed her mind by then. However, your strong reaction may spur her on to keep these ideas in reaction/rebellion to you!

Boyfriend advice. The bits of advice I have given have backfired. So now she wants to ask a therapist or rather friends as she thinks my advice is 'wrong'!

In this situation you could ask her what she thinks her choices are and what are friends believe and then support her to find a middle way through. Try to find neutral in every situation and then you start with an open mind and maybe you will learn more about your daughter as you explore options together.

She met with a therapist before going to boarding school, who she got along very well with and now wants to speak to regularly. We question now why she needs to speak to her when we know the other children who meet the same therapist have REAL problems. She says she "can talk about anything to her and she does not judge me". I want to avoid the therapist eating into our window of communication and closeness. How do we rationalise this?

It sounds like the therapist has provided the space for your daughter to feel at ease, you can now expand on this; whether that is to talk to establish the need follow therapy, to ask your daughter and the therapist if you can share a session to talk through issues together with a therapist/mediator. In your daughter's head she is experiencing problems, and even though to you they are not as 'real' as others to her they are clearly causing issues and can lead to more. You made the right call to send her to therapy and now to integrate the therapy supporting you all.

Reflections, where to from here

I hope that this book has allowed you to explore elements of how you are and who you are as a person, a parent and how to understand and change the behaviour/reactions that no longer serve you, your relationship with your teenager and your family. Life can be fast paced, furious and full on and we can get so lost and overwhelmed by all we think we should be; should be doing or should have that we can lose the texture and quality of life. We neglect the very basics! We can get so caught up in the 'doings' of life that 'being' is stressful, reactive and life becomes a daily challenge or feels relentless!

So, what is it you want 'to be' within your life right now?

What is it you want to feel?

What do you want to put into your most important relationships?

What is it you want to get from life?

What are your intentions for change?

How can you see yourself putting those changes into place?

Who could help support you do this, make the changes?

How can you do one thing daily that creates the habit of changes, that takes you closer to your goal?

What else do you need to make the changes easier?

How can you help yourself make these changes easier?

We are all on this journey of life, we all struggle with elements of our life, we can all feel like we are winging it on a regular basis, it is up to us to choose to have the courage or the commitment to make changes that create a better quality of life, of relationships, enhanced boundaries, of self-awareness and self- care.

It is important to be a role model to our children (our greatest and most important achievements and the next generation) as to what a good, healthy, loving and kind life looks like. Our legacy is to ensure that we have allowed our kids to know that we are all works of art in progress, that life is a journey of discovery, healing, exploring and one where we can recognise the power of who we are on a daily basis and that each day can be a gift. If we allow ourselves to recognise no matter how tough life gets that not everyone has the chance at another day, another opportunity to grow, to change, to accept and to become more of whom we can be.

Life can be challenging, add to the mix, mental health issues, relationship issues, jobs, exams, school pressures, friendships, hormones, brain growth, illness' bills, to do lists and you have the pressure of just surviving. We have a responsibility to teach our kids that sometimes life can feel like survival and whilst sometimes we can thrive, sometimes we might want to give up on everything and that is alright and sometimes we will feel like we are flying, so the aim of this book is to be ok with where ever you are and know that this too will change…

"When we accept ourselves for where we are then we have the power to change.", Carl Jung

To allow ourselves the permission we need to be, to find the information we need to feel where we are and to put into place whatever it is we need to grow and to change to give ourselves permission to 'un-become' and at the same time 'become' and as we choose to do this we role model to our kids that life is ever changing and so too are we

Make your journey through life, be one that allows you to become more of the person you want to be, to feel more of the feelings that enhance you, to experience more of what allows you happiness. Give yourself permission to be the most loving you for YOU, and that in turn gives everyone you love that same gift!

What is the next step that you feel would allow you to use the pause? The step that would allow for calmer communications, that supports you to see yourself, your teen(s) and your family creating a calmer and healthier way through these transformative years!

Daily Care Plan

In order to be a calmer, healthier person, what is it that you need to support you each day? It may be a routine, exercise, headspace, vitamins, quiet or a walk.
EXPLORE what supports you to feel more you and then drop it into your day.

MORNINGS
Starting your day well...

1)

2)

3)

4)

5)

EVENINGS
Ending the day and decompressing to support good sleep and relaxation...

1)

2)

3)

4)

5)

NEXT STEPS
what is it that I want to change within myself that will support relationships within my family.

1)

2)

3)

How will I make these changes?

How do I see this working out and what do I need to do to make it happen?

Who can I ask to help, support, remind me?

What are the stages?

What is the outcome?

How will it feel when all is resolving, healing?

How will I know it is healing?

Acknowledgements

There are so many people that have played a pivotal role in the creation of this book and without whom I would not have had the courage, belief or confidence to bring this together.

I want to thank each and every client who has had the courage to bare their soul, their fears, feelings and their most true self in therapy, it takes a brave person to sit with their truth and to want to heal the pain and confusion. To each and every parent who showed up for their child by bringing them to therapy, I honour you and the unconditional love and strength you have and had to start the process to find clarity and calm for your child as they were going through crisis. I feel so deeply honoured to work in therapy, with the people that I work and have worked with. I love that each day I learn more about people, love, fear, feelings, the human mind, heart, the human condition and how life impacts us all in so many different ways. Every day I get to connect to people in a beautifully authentic and real way.

To all the teenagers that I have the luxury to support, you give me the gift of insight into your world, that I know is difficult and challenging but you still show up and share the confusion of being you in a world that can feel deeply overwhelming and made more difficult sometimes by us, the parents, trying to do our best and not always succeeding!

To my teenagers, TnT, you are a constant learning curve for

me and being your mother has and is the biggest most incredible journey, one where I make take a few wrong turnings, detours and go completely the opposite way to the sat nav, but I hope you know that this book would not be as it is if it wasn't for you showing me each and every day that the PAUSE is a vital tool and that love doesn't always mean we act in the best way! Thank you too for all the insights into how the book and title could be and thank you to the eldest T for the final edit too!

To my friends and family who supported me as I became more and more consumed by this project, to Victoria, for being number one reader, Claire for being the initial inspirer, Liz and Susan for reading and rereading, for Sarah for not reading, Sally Ann without you this would have been a very different journey, Lee your insights have only enhanced it, Amanda thank you for mirroring back to me self-belief, Jo, Lolly and Mark your support means the world.

To Angel, C B, Charlie, D E, J B, H D and Sadie, thank you for sharing your truths. To the parents' input, thank you for your insights and honesty.

To my husband, parents and Joshua who have inspired me to be the mother I am today without you I wouldn't be me.

Thank you too for the gift of motherhood that is a role that is too easily taken for granted. It is a miracle some women have to fight for or never get to appreciate and for me it is a journey that I was never sure I would be lucky enough to travel. It is not an easy journey, but it is one that I know has changed me and allowed me to become more truly me!

Lightning Source UK Ltd.
Milton Keynes UK
UKHW012044290620
365756UK00002B/101